GR

Chocolate

around the

World

Featuring.....

- Nearly 300 brands
- In 66 countries
- Across 6 continents

GG Grahame's
Guides

Web Guides International LLC | New York

Copyright © 2021
Web Guides International LLC
All Rights Reserved.

Grahame's Guides™ is an imprint of
Web Guides International LLC.

This book or parts thereof may not be reproduced in any form, stored in any retrieval system, or transmitted in any form by any means—electronic, mechanical, photocopy, recording, or otherwise—without prior written permission of the publisher, except as provided by United States of America copyright law.

While we have sought to provide accurate, up-to-date information, it is subject to change and error. Please check directly with chocolate company directly as to food allergies or other issues that may concern you.

Printed in the United States of America

ISBN-13: 978-1-7327005-4-3

Web Guides International LLC
57 West 57th Street, 4th floor
New York, NY 10019
info@grahamesguides.com
www.GrahamesChocolateGuide.com

CONTENTS

INTRODUCTION

Few things unite the world as much as food – and few foods give rise to such unified joy and delight as chocolate.

What is it about this lush, intensively flavorful treat that elicits pleasure to so many people in every corner of the world?

Consider for a moment that virtually every country has enthusiastic consumers of chocolate. What is even more impressive is how many countries produce their own: some 70 countries by our count (and probably more).

To honor this great passion, we have created a compilation of great chocolates around the world. Please note that this is our initial survey – and while it is fairly comprehensive, no doubt we have left out additional brands that we may well want to add in future editions.

In fact, you are welcome to help us by pointing out any ones that you love and would like to recommend. Please feel free to write to us here at listings@grahamesguides.com.

Thank you, and now we hope you will please enjoy your explorations of this guide book.

CHOCOLATE:
A BRIEF HISTORY

1,500 BC	Olmec Indians are believed to have grown the first crop of cocoa beans.
250-900 AD	The Mayans adopt many of the Olmec traditions, including the consumption of "xocolatl" as an unsweetened drink. The cocoa bean also assumes an important role as a currency.
1200	The Mayans pass along their knowledge of cacao to the Aztecs who call it "cacahuatl" and flavor it with such spices as chile, cinnamon, pepper, and vanilla. The Aztecs also believe it is a gift given to them from the god Quetzalcoatl.
1502	On his fourth visit to the New World, Christopher Columbus is offered cacao beans by the locals and brings them back to King Ferdinand.
1519	Explorer Hernando Cortés sets foot in Mexico and finds the Aztecs drinking a red, bitter drink made with cocoa called Xocoatl. Recognizing its value, both medicinal and monetary, he begins sending it back to Spain.
1590	Spanish monks create the first sweet chocolate drink, adding honey, vanilla and sugar to it so as to better fit with Spanish tastes.

1606	Italian Antonio Carletti, upon visiting the Spanish Colonies, discovers this wondrous bean and brings it back to Florence where it soon spreads to Venice, Turin and other major cities.
1615	France discovers cocoa when Spanish Princess Maria Theresa marries Louis XIV and gives him an engagement gift of chocolate. It is consumed as a hot drink among the aristocracy and upper classes.
1641	Germany learns of chocolate when scientist Johann Voldkammer discovers it in Naples and brings it home where it becomes popular as a bedtime drink.
1657	The English are introduced to the cocoa bean when the first chocolate house opens its doors in London, serving an "excellent West India drink."
1670	In Boston, Dorothy Jones and Jane Barnard successfully petition the city "to keepe a house of publique Entertainment for the sellinge of Coffee and Chucalettoe."
1728	The Fry family sets up the first chocolate factory in the UK, using hydraulic machinery and equipment to process and grind cocoa beans.
1737	Swedish naturalist Carolus Linnaeus gives cacao its scientific name of "theobroma," which in Greek means "food of the gods."

1828	Dutchman Coenraad Van Houten invents a revolutionary cocoa press which separates cocoa solids from cocoa butter. The defatted powder is easily dissolved in liquids.
1848	Joseph Fry creates the first chocolate bar, known as "eating chocolate," by adding back melted cacao butter.
1861	British merchant Richard Cadbury introduces the first-ever heart-shaped box of chocolates, especially for Valentine's Day.
1875	Switzerland's Daniel Peter creates the first milk chocolate by adding in a milk powder.
1879	Another Swissman, Rodolphe Lindt, invents the "conching" machine, which improves chocolate's taste and texture.
1900	Milton Hershey sells his caramel business to focus on chocolate and a few years later creates the "Hershey Kiss."
1912	In Belgium, Jean Neuhaus fills a chocolate shell with cream and nut pastes – and thus the praline is born.
1947	Canadian children stage a broad boycott after discovering that the chocolate bar's price had risen from 5 to 8 cents.
1950s	In the post-war period, chocolate sees a massive growth in consumption, becoming a part of many people's regular eating habits.

CHOCOLATE
FACTS & NUMBERS

1 billion	The number of cacao plants around the world.
5 to 7	The number of years a farmer must wait for a cacao plant to produce its first beans.
40%	Cote d'Ivoire is the single largest producer of cocoa, providing about 40% of the world's supply.
93°F	The temperature at which chocolate melts -- just below body temperature, which is why it melts so easily on your tongue.
600	The number of flavor compounds in chocolate. By comparison, wine has just 200.
800	The tons of chocolate sold by venders at Brussels Airport each year, making it the biggest chocolate seller in the world.
12,770	The weight of the largest-ever chocolate bar, created by Thornton's of Great Britain on its 100th anniversary.

Top chocolate PRODUCERS	Cote d'Ivoire, Ghana, Indonesia, Nigeria, Cameroon, Brazil, Ecuador, Mexico, Peru, and the Dominican Republic.

Top chocolate CONSUMERS	Switzerland, Germany, Austria, Ireland, United Kingdom, Norway, Estonia, Sweden, Kazakhstan, Slovakia.

Theobroma	This is the scientific name for the tree that chocolate comes from. It means "food of the gods."

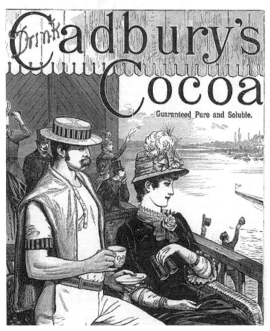

1885 Ad for Cadbury's

DID YOU KNOW....

o   Each pod on a cacao tree contains about 40 beans – and it takes about 500 beans to produce just one pound of chocolate.

o   The amount of chocolate a country consumes correlates to the number of Nobel Laureates it produces.

o   German chocolate cake is not from Germany but rather was named for Sam German, who developed a sweet bar.

o   "Baker's Chocolate" is named after Dr. James Baker who, along with John Hannon, founded a chocolate company in 1765.

o   Chocolate gives you a more intense mental high and gets your heart pounding more than kissing does.

o   A 2013 study found that the scent of chocolate in a bookstore made customers 40% more likely to buy cookbooks or romance novels -- and 22% more likely to buy books of any kind.

THE
GLOBAL
CHOCOLATES

While much of this guide features smaller, regional chocolate brands, we recognize here some of the global giants that daily keep millions of chocolate consumers happy the world over:

Cadbury	Beloved for its delicious milk chocolate, Cadbury is truly one of the grand-daddies of chocolate history. Started in Birmingham, England, in 1824 by John Cadbury, today it operates in more than 50 countries. www.cadbury.co.uk
Dove	Born in Chicago in the 1930s, the Dove brand (known as Galaxy in some countries) has blossomed into a much-consumed and enjoyed brand throughout the world. Since 1986, it has been owned by Mars. www.marschocolate.com/dove
Ferrero Rocher	Launched in 1942 by Pietro Ferrero in Alba, Italy, the Ferrero Rocher company produces its gold-wrapped chocolates today for consumers all around Europe, the U.S. and other parts of the world. www.ferrerorocher.com

Godiva	This famous Belgian chocolate, named for an English noblewoman, got its start in 1926 in the Brussels workshop of Pierre Draps Sr. and his three sons. Since then, it has spread its joy to chocolate lovers inover 100 countries. www.godiva.com
Hershey	In Pennsylvania in 1894, after first making caramels, Milton Hershey tried his hand at cocoa and it was a winner! Then came chocolates, his famous kisses and much, much more. The rest, so to speak, is chocolate history. www.hersheys.com
Lindt & Sprüngli	In 1845, Zurich's David Sprüngli-Schwarz got the bright idea to make chocolate in solid form. Today, his bars are sold in over 120 countries around the world; plus, they've acquired other popular brands, such as Ghirardelli, Cafferel, and Russell Stover. www.lindt-spruengli.com
Toblerone	This famed chocolate maker got its start in Bern, Switerland, in 1868. But it was not until 1908 that founder Jean Tobler's son, together with his cousin, invented the triangular-shaped bar known throughout the world today. www.toblerone.com

Abbreviation Key

Chocolates with the following notations offer at least *some* products of this kind, according to our research. However, to be 100% certain, please be sure to contact the chocolate maker directly for confirmation.

🫘	Bean to Bar
FT	Fair Trade
GF	Gluten Free
K	Kosher
🌿	Organic
⊠	Sugar Free
V	Vegan

Please note: Brief quotations in the listings are from company websites to help provide insight into their approach and processes.

EUROPE

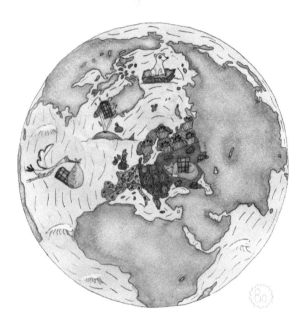

AUSTRIA

Austrians certainly love their chocolate! Emperor Charles VI is said to have introduced it to Vienna when the moved his court there from Madrid. The Viennese soon found delightful ways to make and consumer Notably, the country is famed for its scrumptious *sacher torte*, invented by Franz Sacher in 1832 and is still prized throughout the country.

Altmann & Kühne

Est.1928 by Emil Altmann and Ernst Kuhne
Am Graben 30
1010 Vienna
Tel: +43 1 533 09 27
www.altmann-kuehne.at

"Delicious individual confections made of nougat, marzipan and cocoa – the destiny of which is to melt tenderly in your mouth."

Heindl

Est.1953 by Walter Heindl
Willendorfer Gasse 2-8
1230 Vienna
Tel: +43 1 667 21 10-0
www.heindl.co.at
FT ✍ V

"Only from the best raw materials and attention to detail, our confectioners can produce those delicacies that are appreciated far beyond."

Schokov

Est.2006 by Thomas Kovazh
Siebensterngasse 20
1070 Vienna
Tel.: +43 664/885 13 145
www.schokov.com

"Schokov was born in 2006 out of a life-long dream…of making people happy with chocolate. And to give each one a piece of the ultimate happiness."

Xocolat

Est. 2009 by Ramona Mahr and Werner Meisinger
Freyung 2
A-1010 Wien
Tel: +43 1 535 43 63
www.xocolat.at

"Chocolate specialties are…from high-quality couvertures, fresh nuts and aromatic fruits, noble distillates and other natural ingredients."

Zotter
Est.1999 by Josef Zotter
Bergl 56
8333 Riegersburg
Tel: +43 3152 5554
www.zotter.at
🌿 FT 🌿 🌿 🍶 ⅄

"Our focus is on variety, quality and innovation, we practice creativity, sustainability and 100% organic and fair trade quality…."

FRY'S Pure Concentrated COCOA.

A DELIGHTFUL BEVERAGE for BREAKFAST or SUPPER.

HALF a TEASPOON-FUL MAKES A DELICIOUS CUP OF COCOA.

HOLD THIS UP TO THE LIGHT.

"The Drink —par excellence— for Children."
Dr. STANLEY.

"I have never tasted Cocoa that I like so well."
Dr. CAMERON.

This Choice Cocoa is prepared by a new and special scientific process, securing extreme solubility, developing the finest flavour of the Cocoa, and producing a thin agreeable beverage. It is very nutritious, and being easily digested, it is specially adapted to Children and Invalids.

SOLUBLE !   EASILY DIGESTED !!   ECONOMICAL !!!

Source: Wellcome Trus

19th century ad from Fry's of Bristol, England

BELGIUM ▮▮

Though small in size, Belgium is one of the biggest producers of chocolate in the world – thanks to a fate of history. When the Spanish occupied the country in the 17th century, they introduced the cocoa bean, which they had brought from South America. At first, chocolate was consumed as a drink by the wealthy. But in the mid-1800s it really took off when Jean Neuhaus introduced the praline.

Belvas
Est.2005 by Theirry Noesen
Chemin du Fundus 7 –
7822 Ghislenghien
Tel: +32 68/33.77.46
www.belvas.be
FT ✍ K ✎ Υ

"All of our ingredients are certified organic…with no hydrogenated fat, no palm oil, no coloring, no preservatives and no artificial flavors."

Café Tasse
Est.1964 by Gembler family
1, avenue Reine Astrid
1440 Wauthier-Braine
Tel: +32 2 366 96 14
www.cafe-tasse.com

"Made in the pure Belgian tradition and conditioned in a noble nature-friendly material. This is how the Café-Tasse chocolate brand [was] born."

Centho
Est.2002 by Els and Geert Decoster
Veeweidestraat 3
3080 Duisburg (Tervuren)
Tel: +32 2 767 07 74
www.centho.com

"Centho…chooses precious ingredients that raise each chocolate above all others… we choose to cover our chocolates with a unique cocoa."

Chocolate Line
Est.1992 by Dom. Persoone, F.de Staercke
Simon Stevinplein 19
8000 Brugge
Tel: +32 50 34 10 90
www.thechocolateline.be
🖤

"Chocolate wouldn't be rock and roll if we didn't try something out of the ordinary….to experiment to our heart's content."

Dolfin
Est.1989 by Michael and
Jean-Francois Poncelet
172 Ave. Robert Schuman
1401 Baulers (Nivelles)
Tel: +32 2 366 24 24
www.dolfin.be
FT

"Dolfin's philosophy has been to mix natural, high quality ingredients directly into the chocolate mass. Fruits, spices, herbs, flowers or even the great classics."

Dumon
Est.1992 by Stepnan Dumon
Aartrijkestraat 93
8820 Torhout
Tel: +32 50/22.16.22
www.chocolatierdumon.be

"What makes us different…the originality of our treats, prepared with only the best raw materials and passion for our business."

Galler
Est.1976 by Jean Galler
Rue au Beurre, 44
1000 Brussels
Tel: +32 2 502 02 66
www.galler.com

"Jean Galler…selects the best ingredients and creates chocolate recipes that somehow express more than the sum of their parts."

Goosens
Est1955 by Rene Goosens
Isabellalei 6
2018 Antwerp
Tel: +32 3 239 13 10
goossens-chocolatier.com

"Two generations of real maître chocolatiers with a passion…that managed to impress royals, presidents and ambassadors around the world."

Leonidas
Est.1913 by Leonidas
Kestekides
Blvd Jules Graindor 41-43
1070 Brussels
Tel: +32 2 522 19 57
www.leonidas.com
K

"Leonidas'…success is based on the virtue of impeccable freshness. Today, Leonidas makes more than 100 varieties…of the highest quality…."

Mary
Est.1919 by Mary Delluc
12 Avenue de Rusatira
1083 Brussels
Tel: +32 2 737 72 41
www.mary.be

"Our artisan chocolatiers hand-craft Mary's Belgian pralines daily, filling them with ganache, praline, caramel, cream, and marzipan."

Ad for French chocolate maker (1893)

Neuhaus
Est.1957 by Jean Neuhaus
Galerie de la Reine
1000 Brussels
Tel: +32 25 68 22 11
www.neuhaus.be
K

"A symphony of taste and texture, made with the finest natural ingredients, composed with the utmost care by our Maîtres Chocolatiers."

Pierre Marcolini
Est.1995 by Pierre Marcolini
R. du bassin Collecteur, 4
1130 Brussels
Tel: +32 25 14 12 06
www.marcolini.be

"I draw inspiration from everywhere: at a modern art exhibition or a conversation amongst friends, or…at a restaurant…most of all it's travelling across the world."

Wittamer
Est.1910 by Henri Wittamer
6 Place du Grand Sablon
1000 Brussels
Tel: +32 25 68 22 11
www.wittamer.com

"Heirs of a long tradition gourmet, Myriam and Paul Wittamer…select and assemble the finest cacao crus to compose delicate marriage of creative flavors."

BULGARIA

Casa Kakau
Est.2016 by Ivan Ilchev
Traiko Kitanchev № 5
Plovdiv 4000
Tel: +359 878 675 780
www.casakakau.com

"We have never produced anything with animal ingredients….We use only natural products, nuts and dried fruits to live up to our slogan – 'Natural & Pure.'"

CYPRUS

Joulietta
Est.2013 by Joulietta James
16A Alexandrou Ipsilandi
Paphos, Cyprus
Tel: +357 70 004 004
www.joulietta.com

"I set about developing… artisan chocolates with the taste of…the Mediterranean island where I live. The… herbs, fruits, and liqueurs on this island inspired me."

CZECH REPUBLIC

Jordi's
Est.2010 by Jiri Stejskal and
Lukas Koudelka
Spitalska 149/7
500 03 Hradec Kralove
Tel: 420 602 305 633
www.jordis.cz

"We import the best cocoa beans available from many countries. Our aim is to make the best chocolate in the world and have fun while doing so."

DENMARK

Cocoa came to be known in Denmark in the 18th century where for years it was seen mostly as a pharmaceutical product. The founders of the earliest Danish chocolatiers were all pharmacists. Of course, that's changed big time and today Denmark offers some of the best chocolate anywhere.

Oialla
Est.2010 by Rasmus Bo Bojese
Ingerslevsgade 60
DK - 1705 Copenhagen V
Tel: +45 3391 4600
www.oialla.com

"Made of wild, organic beans from cocoa trees growing in the jungle of Bolivia...in the purest imaginable form and...controlled all the way from bean to bar."

Peter Beier
Est.1996 by Linda and Peter Beier
Ørsholtvej 35
3000 Helsingør
Tel: +45 4917 0026
www.pbchokolade.dk

"100% handmade using cocoa beans from our own plantation, and ingredients from Ørsholt Estate. The taste experience is always our main focus."

Summerbird
Est.1986 by Mikael Gronlykke
Kronprinsensgade 11
1114 København K
Tel: +45 6371 0204
www.summerbird.dk

"Founded in 1986 by Lene and Sven Grønlykke and their son Mikael… gastronomic pioneers in Denmark…ahead of their time of ideas and thoughts."

Svenningsen
Est.2012 by Jacob Vahr Svenningsen
Vandtårnsvej 104
2860 Søborg
Tel: +45 2335 3373
www.svenningsen.com

"Svenningsen constantly strives…to promote and accentuate the divine nuances of good chocolate, he is innovative and uncompromising."

FINLAND +

It can get pretty cold in Finland! Never fear. They have had their trusted sources of chocolate to help keep them warm for many years now. Some of the newest chocolatiers like the two below are also among the most cutting edge.

Goodio
Est.2014 by Jukka Peltola
Kaikukatu 4
00530 Helsinki
Tel: +358 45181 2270
www.goodiochocolate.com

"Created on the principles of sustainability, well-being, and transparency. It's a vision to bring Nordic-inspired flavors…for the global consumer."

Mercedes
Est.2003 by Mercedes Windquist
Aland
Tel: +350 40 539 6699
www.chocolaterie.ax

"Mercedes lives in the Aland Islands… experimenting with new taste combinations… decorating them, and placing them pretty in their boxes."

FRANCE ▮▮

As early as 1609, Portuguese Jewish traders, returning from travels to South America, brought cocoa beans to the Basque city of Bayonne. There they developed a process of roasting them in ovens and then crushing them so they might be used to make a hot drink. From then on, chocolate only became more and more popular. Marie Antoinette even had her own chocolate maker at Versailles. Today, of course, France boasts some of the world's best-admired chocolatiers.

A. Morin
Est.1884 by Gustave Morin
640 Chemin du Plan
26290 Donzère
Tel: +33 (0)4 75 51 60 76
www.chocolaterie-morin.com

"The range of chocolates offered highlights cocoas from different parts of the world, from different plantations, all with unique aromatic profiles."

Alain Ducasse
Est.1996 by Alain Ducasse
40 Rue de la Roquette
75011 Paris
Tel: +33 1 48 05 05 72
lechocolat-alainducasse.com

"Alain Ducasse and Nicolas Berger select their cacao beans based on purity and personality…from a dozen locations, resulting in as many identities and unique flavors."

Bernachon
Est. 1953 by Maurice Bernachon
42 Cours Franklin Roosevelt
69006 Lyon
Tel: +33 4 78 24 37 98
www.bernachon.com

"The children of Françoise and Jean-Jacques Bernachon…have taken over the company…with the tradition and passion that make Bernachon today."

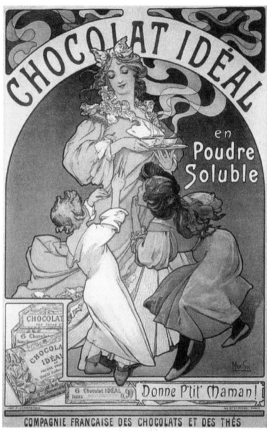

19ᵗʰ century French advertisement

Bonnat
Est. 1983 by Raymond
Bonnat
8 cours Senozan
38502 Voiron
Tél: +33 4 76 05 28 09
bonnat-chocolatier.com
K

"When you first taste Bonnat chocolate, expect the unexpected, a showcase of flavours, and pure, velvety sensations of pleasure."

Bouga Cacao

Est.2996 by Ulrike Bongartz
Moragues – La Vigne
09000 Foix
Tel: +33 5 61 65 54 12
www.bouga-cacao.com

"Bouga Cacao is… the story of a real passion for excellent cocoa beans…. based on the direct cooperation with our partners in Ecuador."

Cadiot-Badie

Est. 1825 by Jean-Emil Vene
26, Allées de Tourny
33000 Bordeaux
Tel: +33 5 56 44 24 22
www.cadiot-badie.com

"Bitterness…without pungency, sweetness… without persistence, barely suggested acidity and sublimation for the aromas, …in delicate nuances."

Castelain

Est. 1954 Bernard Castelain
Route de Sorgues
84230 Châteauneuf du Pape
Tel: +33 4 90 83 54 71
www.castelainchocolat.com
FT

"Located in the heart of the vineyards of Chateauneuf-du-Pape…we offer…the classic chocolate bar… chocolate candies and essential specialties."

Christophe Roussel

Est. 2004 by Chrisophe
Roussel
5 rue tardieu
75018 Paris
Tel: 01 42 58 91 01
www.christophe-roussel.fr

"Full of ideas and creativity, Christophe Roussel makes delicious pastries, macarons and chocolates with the best ingredients. His credo: simplicity and generosity."

Debauve & Gallais

Est. 1800 by Sulpice
Debauve
6 Rue Brûlée
67000 Strasbourg
Tel: +33 3 69 57 68 19
www.debauve-et-gallais.fr

"Bite into one of our chocolate pastilles and you'll find yourself rubbing shoulders with Marie-Antoinette in 1779."

"All you need is love. But a little chocolate now and then doesn't hurt."
-- Charles M. Schulz

Erithaj

Est. 2013 by Arnaud Stengel
6 rue Brûlée
67000 Strasbourg
Tel: +33 1 70 39 38 00
www.erithaj.com

"Arnaud Stengel… has put his signature in the world of chocolate, creating Erithaj… promoting a direct relationship with the families of planters."

Jean-Paul Hévin

Est. 1988 by Jean-Paul Hevin
23 Ave de la Motte Picquet
75007 Paris
Tel: +33 1 45 51 45 99
www.jeanpaulhevin.com

"With the very best ingredients collected from around the world, Jean-Paul Hevin and his team develop new chocolate confections."

Maison du Chocolat

Est. 1977 by Robert Linxe
41-43 rue Paul Lescop
92000 Nanterre
Tel: +33 1 55 51 83 18
lamaisonduchocolat.com

"La Maison du Chocolat has transformed the world of chocolate, introducing vibrant creativity inspired by the vision of founder Robert Linxe."

Patrick Roger

Est. 1997 by Patrick Roger
108, Blvd Saint-Germain
75006 Paris
Tel. +33 1 43 29 38 42
www.patrickroger.com

"It all starts with an emotion, the unconscious...a material, a smell, a person…Creating is not enough. You must pick and choose the best taste."

Pierre Hermé

Est. 1998 by Pierre Herme
72, rue de Bonaparte
75006 Paris
Tel. +33 1 45 12 24 02
www.pierreherme.com

"With "pleasure as his only guide," Pierre Hermé has invented a totally original world of tastes, sensations and pleasures."

Pralus

Est. 2000 by François Pralus
34, rue Général Giraud
42300 Roanne
Tel: +33 4 77 68 99 36
www.chocolats-pralus.com

"Pralus works with dried cocoa beans…from the very best cocoa plantations all over the world. From these…he produces around 15 pure varieties."

Richart

Est. 1925 Joseph Richart
27 rue Bonaparte
75006 Paris
Tel. +33 1 56 81 16 10
www.richart.com

"A family tradition of ceaseless pursuit of perfection….You'll enjoy a peerless mix of innovation, purity, elegance and clean design."

Ad for Parisian chocolate maker (1890)

GERMANY

Chocolate came to Germany in the early 1600s, first as a medicine in pharmacies and later as a drink. However, because of its high price and import tariffs, it was considered a luxury good reserved for the aristocracy and affluent. One early promoter, Prince Wilhelm von der Lippe, built the first chocolate factory. Today, Germans are the second-largest consumers of chocolate per capita after the Swiss.

Belyzium
Est. 2014 by Andrei Shibkov
Lottumstrasse 15
10119 Berlin
Tel: +49 30 4404 6484
www.belyzium.com

"We do everything…we grow and process cacao in Belize, ship the beans to Germany and make Bean to Bar organic chocolate right in the center of Berlin!"

Clement
Est. 2001 by Franz Clement
Hackenstraße 3
80331 München
www.clement-chococult.de

"Franz X. Clement focused on the quality of the raw materials and the taste of the cakes and pralines. Great value is always placed on the craft."

Coppeneur
Est.1993 by Oliver Coppeneur
Gewerbepark Dachsberg 1
53604 Bad Honnef
Tel: +49 2224 9010-40
www.coppeneur.de

"Our passion is to reflect cocoa and chocolate in all its facets and process them into enjoyable compositions using the finest natural raw materials."

Evers & Tochter
Est. 1925 Joseph Richart
Breite Strasse 9
23552 Lübeck
Tel: +49 451 39 68 538
www.eversundtochter.com

"In our manufactory…we create jewels made of flowers and chocolate to amaze you. Our assortment carries the finest chocolate …with the highest standards."

Georgia Ramon
Est.2015 by Georg Bernardini
and Ramona Gustmann
Königswinterer Str. 624
53227 Bonn
Tel: +49 228 36036886
www.georgia-ramon.com

"We focus on quality, creativity and diversity…. Classics form the basis of our work. In addition, we would also like to create new taste experiences: A vegan chocolate with beetroot & coconut…."

Vivani
Est. 2000 by Andreas Meyer
Diebrocker Str. 17
D-32051 Herford
Tel: +49 234 544 49360
www.vivani-chocolate.de

"We use only the finest organically grown ingredients, the best recipes, proficiency and skill combined with the most up-to-date production equipment."

*A share of David Söhne, one of Germany's
oldest chocolate makers (1916)*

GREECE

Alexandros

Est. 1999 Alexandros
Dimitriou
21 Menexedon Street
14564 Kifissia, Athens
Tel: +30 210 5785859
alexandroschocolates.gr

"Following a specialized education…in Italy and France, Alexandros… returned to Greece with a vision to highlight the complexity of chocolate."

HUNGARY

Sweets are an essential part of Hungarian cuisine, from tortes to strudels and cakes – and most definitely chocolate. That includes such old-time chocolatiers as well as newcomers alike.

Ghraoui

Est. 1996 Bassam Ghraoui
31 Andrássy Avenue
1061 Budapest
Tel: +36 1 398 8791
www.ghraouichocolate.com

"The Ghraoui name is the legacy of an ancient Damascene trading family …The Ghraoui brand has always been associated with high quality."

Rózsavölgyi

Est. 2004 by Zsolt Szabad
and Katalin Csiszar
Királyi Pál u. 6
1053 Budapest
Tel: +36 30 683 1228
www.rozsavolgyi.com

"We use traditional processes and pure ingredients to achieve the most natural flavors and …contemporary designs to create…a true piece of art."

ICELAND

Omnom

Est. 2013 Kjartan Gíslason
and Óskar Þórðarson
Hólmaslóð 4
101 Reykjavík
Tel: +354 519 5959
www.omnomchocolate.com

"Chocolate is the labor of a lot of patience, from growing the cacao pods until the bar is safely melting in your mouth …we have been crafting our skill."

IRELAND

Butlers

Est. 1932 by Marion Butler
24 Wicklow Street
Dublin 2   D01 Y364
Tel: +353 1 878 3402
www.butlerschocolates.com

"Butlers…began life…in 1932…founded by a pioneering lady called Marion Butler…making her delicious confections by hand….it is 100% Irish."

Chez Emily

Est. 1996 by Ferd. Vandaele
and Helena Hemeryck
Coolquoy Common
Co. Dublin
Tel: +353 1 835 2252
www.chezemily.ie

"Established in 1996, through a love of all things chocolate, Chez Mily combines the very best raw materials, the freshest local ingredients."

Hazel Mountain

Est. 2014 by Kasha Connolly
9 Middle Street
Galway City
Tel: +353 65 707 8847
hazelmountainchocolate.com

"Our boutique bean to bar chocolate factory and shop in the Burren Mountains is one of the smallest and most remote chocolate factories in the world…."

Lily O'Brien's

Est. 1997 by Mary Ann O'Brien
Newbridge Business Park
Newbridge, Co. Kildare
Tel: +353 45 485 800
www.lilyobriens.ie

"Mary Ann honed her chocolate-making skills among world class chefs and chocolatiers in South Africa and Europe before starting her own mini enterprise from her Kildare kitchen."

Lorge

Est. 1995 by Benoit Lorge
Bonane, Kenmare
Co. Kerry
Tel: +353 64 667 9994
www.lorge.ie

"Benoit…prides himself in following the traditions of the true French artisan.... Inspiration… comes from both the stunning Caha Mountains, lakes and bays."

Wilkie's

Est. by Shana Wilkie
Nordic Enterprise Park
Knockgriffin, Midleton, Cork
Tel: +353 87 699 6454
www.wilkieschocolate.ie

"We are an artisan producer of quality organic dark chocolate, using only the most sustainable and natural ingredients."

Cover art for an old Italian chocolate tin

ITALY

Florentine explorer Antonio Carletti is said to have visited Guatemala in the 1590s, discovered their cocoa plantations, and brought word of this wondrous bean back to his Medici benefactors. Its popularity soon grew so much that a cardinal in Rome was asked to decide if its consumption was permitted during Lent. His decision: yes! Today some of the word's finest chocolates can be found throughout Italy.

Amedei
Est. 199 by Cecilia Tessieri
Via San Gervasio, 29
Loc La Rotta – 56025
Pontedera (PI)
Tel: +39 0587 484849
www.amedei.it

"It all began with an idea and a desire to find the world's best cocoa bean in order to produce the most exquisite chocolate possible."

Bodrato
Est. 1943 by Luciano Bodrato
Strada del Turchino, 41
15067, Novi Ligure (AI)
Tel: +39 0143 468902
www.bodratocioccolato.it

"We produce in small batches to ensure the maximum freshness and flavor of the finished product, taking care of every detail."

Bonajuto
Est.1880 by Francesco Bonajuto
Corso Umberto I
159 – 97015 Modica
Tel: +39 0932 941225
www.bonajuto.it

"With more than 150 years of activity, the Dolceria Bonajuto is the oldest chocolate factory in Sicily… and one of the oldest in Italy."

Caffarel
Est.1926 by Pierre Paul Caffarel
Via Gianavello 41
10062 Luserna S. Giovanni
Torino
Tel: +39 0121 958111
www.caffarel.com

"In 1826 Pier Paul Caffarel arrived in Turin with his passion for chocolate and the dream to open his own lab….Now it is close to its 200th birthday!"

Domori
Est. 1997 by Gianluca Franzoni
Via Pinerolo 76
10060 None, Torino
Tel: +39 0119 863465
www.domori.com
FT

"To go where no one has ever been with chocolate, rescuing the pure essence of the noble cocoa, is Domori's passion."

Gay-Odin
Est. 1900 by Isidoro Odin
Via Vetriera 12
80100 Napoli
Tel: +39 195 25 074
www.gay-odin.it

"In the late 1800s begins the journey of the 23-year-old from Alba, en route to Naples… which will inspire his most sought-after creations."

"Forget love…I'd rather fall in chocolate." -- Unknown

Guido Gobino
Est.1964 by Giuseppe Gobino
Via Cagliari 15/b
10153 Torino
Tel: +39 0112 476245
www.guidogobino.com

"Guido Gobino is a craftsman who has innovated…through the careful selection of raw materials…and continuous experimentation."

Roberto Catinari
Est. 1974 by Roberto Catinari
Via Provincale
378 Agliana (Pt)
Tel: +39 0574 718506
www.robertocatinari.it

"Taste our wide range of chocolates, we are sure you will recognize the hand of those who love chocolate and treat it with true passion."

Slitti
Est. 1969 by Andrea Slitti
Via Francesa Sud, 1268
51015 Monsummano Terme
Tel: +39 0572 640240
www.slitti.it

"Slitti was established in 1969 …Andrea is quite a stickler for the best ingredients, he uses only cocoa mass, cocoa butter, sugar and natural vanilla."

Venchi
Est. 1878 by Silviano Venchi
Via dei Mercanti
20123 Milano
Tel: +39 0171 791672
www.venchi.com

"The Venchi story began in the far-off 1800s....in the Piedmont region, Silviano Venchi was an ambitious, creative young man with a great passion for chocolate."

LITHUANIA

Naïve
Est. 2010 by Domantas
Uzpalis
Zietelos 3
Vilnius LT-316
Tel: +370 620 69979
www.chocolatenaive.com

"Naive makes chocolate in ways that help to reveal the character of a...cacao bean. The chocolate is...born after a meticulous analysis of taste, color, smell and texture."

LUXEMBOURG

Genaveh
Est. 2005
52 Rue de Koerich
8437 Steinfort
Tel: +352 27 62 16 17
chocolaterie-genaveh.com
K ☒

"Génaveh is known worldwide for the outstanding quality and presentation of its products: ganaches, caramels, fruit and pralinés fillings."

Oberweis
Est. 1964 by Pit and
Monique Oberweis
1, rue G. Kroll
L-1882 Luxembourg
Tél: +352 40 31 40-1
www.oberweis.lu

"Pit and Monique, then their two sons Tom and Jeff, have put their know-how and creativity to work...with rare authenticity and particular attention to detail."

MONACO

Chocolaterie de Monaco

Est. 1878 by Silviano Venchi
Place de la Visitation
Monaco-Ville 98000
Tel: +377 97 97 88 88
chocolateriedemonaco.com

"An institution devoted to idealize the chocolate, gift of nature and to perpetuate the sacred values of friendship, labor, peace, harmony and respect for nature."

Early 20th Century Dutch advertisement

NETHERLANDS

Give thanks to Dutch inventor Coenraad Van Houten who in 1828 created a revolutionary cocoa press that produces a fine cocoa powder. His contribution enhanced the chocolate-making process, making it easier and cheaper to spread chocolate to the world. Here's to Conraad!

Chocolatemakers
Est. 2011 by Enver Loke and Rodney Nikkels
Zesde Vogelstraat 54
1022 XE Amsterdam
Tel: +31 20 737 26 59
www.chocolatemakers.nl
 FT

"We do everything ourselves in our own factory in Amsterdam….in the traditional way…top quality, with as few additions as possible."

Original Beans
Est. 2008 by Philipp Kauffmann
Keizersgracht 452
1016 GD Amsterdam
www.originalbeans.com
FT

"Founded on a passion for making the finest chocolate and for replenishing what we consume…preserve rare cacaos, protect endangered wildlife…."

Puccini Bomboni
Est. 1987 by Ans van Soelen
Staalstraat 17
1011 JK Amsterdam
Tel: +31 20 626 54 74
www.puccinibomboni.com
FT

"For now almost 30 years we are creating… chocolates in our own kitchen…dedicated to creating the most beautiful tastes and shapes."

Van Soest
Est.2008 by Franny Van Soest
Utrechtsestraat 143
Frederiksplein 1A
1017XK Amsterdam
Tel: +31 20 620 80 25
vansoest-amsterdam.nl
FT

"Van Soest is proud of the chocolate creations that are made artisanally... only fair chocolate and the very best ingredients are used…."

NORWAY

Craig Alibone

Est. 2016 by Craig Alibone
Storgata 3
8006 Sentrumsgarden
Bodø
Tel: +47 755 600 60
www.craigalibone.com

"Craig's aim is to provide the highest quality cakes, macarons and chocolate for all occasions. Each piece is individually handmade to ensure great results."

Sebastien Bruno

Est. 2001 by Sebastien and Bruno
Stenersgaten 1
0050 Oslo
Tel: +47 400 32 510
www.sebastienbruno.no

"Chocolate from Sebastien Bruno is handmade, has a high cocoa content, has no preservatives and contains very little sugar. The result is an exclusive selection."

Vigdis Rosenkilde

Est. 2012 by Vigdis Rosenkilde
Heimdalsgata 9
0561 Oslo
Tel: +47 926 64 614
www.rosenkilde.no

"Vigdis is passionately interested in cocoa….She has made fresh chocolate truffles with everything from herbs, blue cheese and raspberries from Sogndal."

French advertisement (circa 1910)

POLAND

Czekolady

Est. 2009 by Tomasz
Sienkiewicz and Krzysztof
Stypulkowski
ul.Marszałkowska 9/15
00-626 Warszawa
Tel: +48 531 006 756
manufakturaczekolady.pl

*"Chocolate is hand-made
directly from freshly-ground
cocoa beans. From start to
finish, the whole process
takes place in the same
plant."*

PORTUGAL

Chocolate as a drink did not catch on as quickly in
Portugal as elsewhere in Europe. They preferred tea
due to their early contact with China. But once
chocolate began to be consumed in blocks, the
Portuguese lost no time in producing their own
amazing creations – as exemplified by these four
historic chocolatiers below:

Arcadia

Est. 1933 by the Bastos
family
Rua do Almada, 63
4050-036 Porto
Tel: +351 222 001 518
www.arcadiachocolates.com

*"One of Arcádia's best kept
secrets is … the choice of
raw material… premium
ingredients, and… century-
old production method. This
is the only way to achieve…
visual and flavor coherence.*

Cacao di Vine

Est. 2013 by Nuno Jorge and
Nuno Andrade
Rua Vale do Paraíso - 31
Coimbra 3040-501
Tel: +351 239 164 134
www.cacaodivine.com

*"This handmade chocolate...
will open your mind and
reveal to you the intense
aromas and fragrances of
each wine."*

Denegro
Est. 2010 by Isabel Leitao
Rua de S. Bento nº333
1250-220 Lisboa
Tel: +351 21 099 8022
www.denegro.pt

"Chocolate, if it is handmade, doesn't hide its origin. The aroma, the flavour, and the way it presents itself, all craftsmanship and dedication is revealed."

Feitoria do Cacao
Est. 2015 by Tomoko Suga
and Sue Tavares
E. de São Bernardo Lj. 91B
3810-195 Aveiro
Tel: +351 234 427 100
www.feitoriadocacao.com

"We make the choice of cocoa, we roast it, part the skins, grind, refine, temper it and pack by hand, from the raw cocoa beans to the finished bar."

"There is nothing better than a friend, unless it is a friend with chocolate."
-- *Linda Grayson*

SLOVAKIA

Lyra
Est. 2008 by Maria Capova
Konecna 2
951 12 Ivanka pri Nitre
Tel: +421 902 117 041
www.lyrachocolate.com

"Making quality chocolate means to know each farmer, each tree, each detail; it means to understand each stage of cocoa's journey."

SPAIN

When conquistador Don Cortés first sampled the "'chocolatl" drink with the Aztecs, he was so impressed that he brought back to Spain the cocoa beans and equipment to process them. His compatriots at home found a more suitable way to consume it: warm and sweetened. For nearly a century, the Spanish kept the special drink all to themselves, but could only keep it a secret for so long. It spread across the European continent – and the rest is chocolate history.

Amatller
Est. 1797 by Gabriel Amatller
Sant Pere, 37
08770 Barcelona
Tel: +34 93 891 11 00
www.chocolateamatller.com

"The Amatller family's dedication… started…when Gabriel…came to Barcelona … creating products that allow us to enjoy chocolate with all our senses."

Blanxart
Est. 1954 by Francesc Agras
Corsega 218
08036 Barcelona
Tel: +34 93 414 26 38
www.blanxart.com

"In April of 1954…master chocolatier Francesc Agrás embarked on a long journey…. founding of one of the most renowned Catalan chocolate factories."

Enric Rovira
Est. 1993 by Enric Rovira
Sant Geroni, 17
08296 Barcelona
Tel: +34 934 160 112
www.enricrovira.com

"Enric Rovira is an enterprise with a lot of experience but young at the same time…. The enterprise is alive proposing new chocolate ideas year after year."

Farga
Est. 1957 by Jesus Farga
Avda. Diagonal 391
08002 Barcelona
Tel: +34 900 878 978
www.fargachocolates.com

"Farga Group has its foundations in the constant search for excellence, supported by values such as Quality, Creativity, Professionalism."

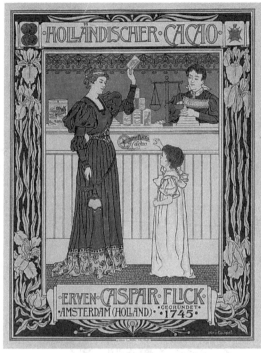

Dutch advertisement (1897)

Oriol Balaguer
Est. 2002 by Oriol Balaguer
Calle Ortega y Gasset, 44
28006 Madrid
Tel: +34 933 632 298
www.oriolbalaguer.com

"Inspired by architecture and the culture of design, Oriol Balaguer produces sweet cuisine based on finely honed artisan techniques and the perfect balance of taste."

Simon Coll
Est. 1840 by Simon Mestres
Sant Pere, 37
08770 Sant Sadurní
d'Anoia
Tel: +34 93 891 11 00
www.simoncoll.com

*"A new generation, the sixth, is now starting to plan a future of innovation
that will continue Simón Coll's long history, faithful to the company's values."*

SWEDEN

Swedes have a sweet tooth aplenty, which shows itself in a great variety of favorite dessert dishes, from crepes and waffles to rice pudding and something altogether unique called *spettekaka*. Yet, chocolate holds a special place too as you will find with these dedicated chocolatiers from throughout the country.

Betsy Sandberg
Est. 1926 by Betsy Sandberg
Nybrogatan 31
114 39 Stockholm
Tel: +46 8 663 63 05
www.betsysandberg.se

"We are a family-run company that has manufactured…in Stockholm since 1926. All according to the small-scale tradition of craftsmanship."

Ejes
Est. 1923 Judith Andersson
Erik Dahlbergsgatan 25
115 32 Stockholm
Tel: +46 8 664 27 09
www.ejeschoklad.se

"With knowledge and traditions since 1923, Ejes chocolate has become one of Sweden's oldest and leading family companies in chocolate and confectionery."

Handgjort
Est. 2005 Anicka Larsson
Hanna Paulis Gata 29
Fruängen
Tel: +46 8 646 89 42
www.handgjortstockholm.se

"At Handgjort you will find… chocolate pralines made with focus on the taste and appearance….Round balls, cut pralines, stuffed shells …and colorful creations."

Malmo
Est. 1888 by Emil Nissen
Möllevångsgatan 32B
214 20 Malmo
Tel: +46 4 045 95 05
malmochokladfabrik.se

"We believe that what chocolate can do for the world is only limited by the boundaries of imagination. If we can dream it, we can do it!"

FT

SWITZERLAND ✚

You can thank Zurich Mayor Heinrich Escher for bringing chocolate to Switzerland in 1697 after learning about it in Brussels. However, it was not until 1819 when an enterprising Francois-Luis Cailler built the country's first chocolate factory. Other great Swiss chocolate pioneers have since followed in their foot steps: Philippe Suchard, Rudolf Sprüngli, Rodolphe Lindt, Jean Tobler, Henri Néstle, and Robert and Max Frey. The Swiss not only enjoy making chocolate. They also rank as the number one per capital consumers in the world.

Eichenberger
Est. 1959 by the
Eichenberger family
Bahnhofplatz 5
3011 Bern
Tel: +41 31 311 33 25
confiserie-eichenberger.ch

"A traditional family business… founded in 1959 and since then has grown steadily….quality and courteous service is the cornerstone of our success."

Favarger
Est. 1826 by Jacques Foulquier
Chem. de la Chocolaterie 2
1290 Versoix
Tel: +41 22 775 11 00
www.favarger.com

"A watchmaker fell in love with the daughter of a chocolate maker. By marrying her, he learnt alongside his father-in-law….Today Favarger remains family-run."

Idilio Origins
Est. 2011 by Pascal Wirth and Niklaus Blumer
Leimenstrasse 47
CH-4002 Basle
Tel: +41 61 270 12 80
www.idilio.ch

"We employ the traditional 'long' conche, which no modern stirring method can match when it comes to gently unfolding the exquisite flavours."

Laderach

Est. 1962 by Rudolph Laderach
Bleiche 14
CH-8755 Ennenda
Tel: +41 55 645 44 44
www.laederach.com

"Läderach has stood for top-quality, hand-made Swiss chocolate specialties since 1962....our family company...is in the canton of Glarus, Switzerland."

Max

Est. 2009 by Patrick Konig
Schweizerhofquai 2
6004 Lucerne
Tel: +41 41 418 70 90
www.maxchocolatier.com
FT ⌀ K ✎ ✗ Ⅴ

"Aromas from trees, jungles and rivers in Asia, South America and the Caribbean make our exclusive single origin chocolates unlike any others."

Sprungli

Est. 1836 David Sprungli
Bahnhofstrasse 21
8001 Zürich
Tel: +41 44 224 46 46
www.spruengli.ch

"For more than 175 years Confiserie Sprüngli has been tempting customers worldwide with their exquisite delicacies … all lovingly made by hand."

Teuscher

Est. 1932 by Dolf Teuscher
Storchengasse 9
CH-8001 Zürich
Tel: +41 44 211 51 53
www.teuscher.com
✗

"More than 80 years ago in a small town in the Swiss Alps, a master chocolate maker embarked on a path that would make him one of the world's greatest."

Commercial poster, Madrid (1890)

UNITED KINGDOM 🇬🇧

Brits somehow lived without chocolate until 1657. That year, the first chocolate house opened its doors, advertising an "excellent West India drink." At first limited to the upper classes, its popularity spread after grocers, such as John Cadbury of Birmingham, began offering it – grinding it right there in the store. A huge step forward took place when Fry's of Bristol began offering chocolate bars. Not to be outdone, Cadbury's sons began selling boxes of chocolates shaped like hearts. Today, British chocolatiers continue to innovate as you'll see from the chocolatiers below:

Artisan du Chocolat

Est.2000 by Gerard Coleman
81 Westbourne Grove
London W2 4UL
Tel: +44 1233 505 170
www.artisanduchocolat.com

"Everything…is about the product…to pay homage to the wonderful crop that is chocolate and to the people who dedicate their life to growing it."

Auberge du Chocolat

Est.2005 by Ann and Ian Scott
28, Chess Business Park
Chesham HP5 1SD
Tel: +44 1494 774 179
www.aubergechocolat.co.uk

"A unique artisan family business….All our hand made products are created with individual care… We love to share our passion for chocolate."

Baravelli's

Est. 2012 by Mark and Emma Baravelli
13 Bangor Road
Conwy LL32 8NG
Tel: +44 1492 330 540
www.baravellis.com

"An innovative hub of all things chocolate….Emma and Mark Baravelli have…been recognised as crafting something very special."

Choc on Choc
Est.2003 by Kerr Dunlop
and Flo Broughton
High Street, Rode
Bath BA11 6PA
Tel: +44 1373 830 160
www.choconchoc.co.uk

"We love being a true British brand offering such a unique range of handmade chocolate…. Designs such as shoes and handbags are big favourites….constant innovation is important ."

Duffy's
Est.2008 by Duffy Sheardown
Humberston Business Park
Humberston DN36 4BJ
Tel: +44 7721 926 706
www.duffyschocolate.co.uk

"We have total control of the roasting and processing of the cocoa beans as we do it all ourselves in Lincolnshire…."

19ᵗʰ century British advertisement for chocolate

www.grahameschocolateguide.com

Green & Black's

Est. 1991 by Craig Sams
and Josephine Fairley
105 Victoria St., Westminster
London SW1E 6QT
Tel: +44 2030 472 523
www.greenandblacks.com
● FT ● γ

"From ingredients like hand harvested Anglesey sea salt and Mediterranean almonds, we take great pride in creating distinctively smooth and rich chocolate..."

Hotel Chocolat

Est.2011 by Angus Thirlwell
4 Monmouth Street
Gr. London WC2H 9HB
Tel: +44 2072 090 659
www.hotelchocolat.com
● ⅙ ● γ

"For over a decade now, our mantra has been "more cocoa, less sugar". This will never change…. It means that in our chocolate, cocoa is the lead ingredient."

Iain Burnett

Est. 2006 by Iain Burnett
Grandtully
Pitlochry PH9 0PL
Tel: +44 1887 840 775
highlandchocolatier.com

"Known as The Highland Chocolatier, Iain Burnett is an award winning artisan based in the heart of the Scottish mountains."

Montezuma's

Est. 2000 Helen and Simon
Pattinson
30 Duke Street
Brighton BN1 1AG
Tel: +44 1273 324 979
www.montezumas.co.uk
FT ⅙ ● γ

"We started…in 2000 with only a kitchen-sink-sized machine, huge enthusiasm, spades of naivety and…a broad ideal to bring chocolate innovation to the boring and staid British chocolate market."

Paul A. Young

Est. 2006 by James Cronin
143 Wardour Street, Soho
London W1F 8WA
Tel: +44 2074 370 011
www.paulayoung.co.uk
●

"Paul has a reputation as an incredibly creative flavour alchemist… original, experimental, sometimes daring, yet always perfectly balanced."

UNITED STATES AND CANADA

CANADA 🍁

Canadians cherish chocolate as much as anyone. It was the Ganong brothers. of New Brunswick who introduced their countrymen to the wrapped chocolate bar in 1910. Canada's children staged a famous boycott in 1947 after discovering that the chocolate bar's price had risen from 5 to 8 cents. Canadians clearly knew what to stand up for! Today, you can find delicious chocolates coast to coast.

Beta5
Est. 2011 by Mark Chandler
413 Industrial Ave.
Vancouver, BC
Tel: 604-669-3336
www.beta5chocolates.com

"A contemporary and innovative chocolate and pastry shop in Vancouver …. constantly influenced by nature and industrial landscapes."

Choklat
Est. 2008 by Brad Churchill
3601B 21 Street NE
Calgary Alberta, T2E6T5
www.choklat.com
Tel: 403-457-1419

"We import the rarest cocoa beans in the world, then roast, grind and refine them into chocolate that meets our exact specifications. This gives us control over the quality and taste."

Christopher Norman
Est. 2009 by Joe Guiliano
Half Moon Bay, BC
Tel: 604-747-4799
www.cnchocolates.com

"Master Chocolatier John Down put his considerable fine arts and design talent to work in the creation of a new genre of hand-made chocolates."

Hummingbird
Est. 2012 by Erica Gilmour
9 Houston Drive
Almonte, ON K0A 1A0
Tel: 613-801-0357
hummingbirdchocolate.com
FT

"There's so much to learn in chocolate; get the right beans – do the right thing – and the flavours unlocked are incredible."

Jacek

Est.2009 by Jacqueline Jacek
406 Kaska Road
Sherwood Park, AB T8A 4G8
Tel: 780-464-5200
www.jacekchocolate.com
🍫 FT Ƴ

"Jacek… was started as a one woman show in late in 2009 in a basement… their quest is to spread joy through fine, fashionable chocolate."

Soma

Est. 2003 by David Castellan
32 Tank House Lane
Toronto, ON M5A 3C4
Tel: 416-815-7662
www.somachocolate.com
🍫 Ƴ

"Curiosity of all things chocolate propels us on as we…seek out great cacao beans…more ingredients, and have nice chats with our regulars and newcomers."

Thomas Haas

Est. 1995 by Thomas Haas
2539 West Broadway
Vancouver, BC V6K 2E9
Tel: 604-736-1848
www.thomashaas.com

"More than 15 years ago, my wife Lisa and I began the journey to…be creative…and…prepare the most delectable handcrafted chocolates."

Lowney's CHOCOLATE BON - BONS

Ad for Boston chocolate maker (circa 1878)

UNITED STATES

Chocolate touched the shores of North America in 1641 aboard a Spanish ship docking in Florida. By the 1700s, the Colonies were importing over 300 tons of cocoa beans and Ben Franklin was selling chocolate in his Philadelphia print shop. In 1849, Domingo Ghirardelli found his own gold mine of sorts from selling chocolate to miners. Thanks to Milton Hershey, it then reached the masses. Now, chocolate making is reaching for amazing innovation as you'll see with these enterprises below.

Arizona

Zak's
Est. 2015 by Jim and Maureen Elitzak
6990 E. Shea Blvd.
Scottsdale AZ 85254
Tel: 480-607-6581
www.zakschocolate.com

"What started as Maureen's home hobby now allows us to share our passion with you…We roast ethically sourced cocoa beans and make our own single-origin and House Blend chocolate. Everything is done by hand."

Arkansas

Kyya
Est. 2012 by Rick and Cindy Boosey
278 North Elm Street
Springdale, AR 72762
Tel: 844-281-4470
www.kyyachocolate.com
FT

"We make small batches of chocolate to maximize the flavor inherent in the single-source cacao beans. No artificial flavors or additives. We built our own supply chain and, where possible, we work directly with our farmers."

California

Chuao

Est. 2002 by Michael Antonorsi
2350 Camino Vida Roble
Carlsbad, CA 92011
Tel: 760-476-0197
www.chuaochocolatier.com

"Michael...founded Chuao...in 2002, naming it as a nod to the legendary cacao-growing region as a reflection of their heritage and commitment to quality."

Compartés

Est. 1950
912 S. Barrington Ave
Los Angeles CA 90049
Tel: 310-826-3380
www.compartes.com

"Compartes has been handcrafting chocolate since 1950 in small batches ...locally sourced ingredients and the best chocolate... around the globe."

"What you see before you, my friend, is the result of a lifetime of chocolate."
-- Katherine Hepburn

Dandelion

Est. 2010 by Cameron Ring and Todd Masonis
740 Valencia Street
San Francisco, CA 94110
Tel: 415-349-0942
dandelionchocolate.com

"Dandelion Chocolate is a bean-to-bar chocolate factory in the Mission District....We roast, crack, sort, winnow, grind, conch, and temper small batches."

Guittard

Est. 1868 by Etienne Guittard
10 Guittard Road
Burlingame, CA 94010
Tel: 800-468-2462
www.guittard.com
FT K

"As the fifth generation joins the company, we continue to ...support, explore and grow with our extended family of customers, co-workers, farmers and suppliers."

John Kelly

Est. 2005 by John Kelson
and Kelly Green
1508 N. Sierra Bonita Ave
Los Angeles, CA 90046
Tel: 800-609-4243
johnkellychocolates.com
K

"Our specialty is exceptionally delicious chocolates. We use all-natural, premium quality ingredients, and make everything in small batches. But it's really all about the level of detail and hand craftsmanship we bring."

LetterPress

Est. 2014 by David and
Corey Menkes
2835 S. Robertson Blvd.
Los Angeles, CA 90034
Tel: 424-240-8580
letterpresschocolate.com
K

"We handcraft our single origin chocolate in small batches, starting with the best cacao beans we can find….Our goal is to forge direct relationships with farmers and co-ops…."

Lulu's

Est. 2006 by Lulu Bonner
419 Broad Street, Ste. A
Nevada City, CA 95959
Tel: 530-264-7058
www.luluschocolate.com
FT Y

"We choose unroasted (raw) cacao in order to maximize cacao's amazing qualities from tree to table. Our cacao is 100% wild-harvested."

Recchiuti

Est. 1997 by Michael
Recchiuti
2565 Third Street
San Francisco, CA 94107
Tel: 800-500-3396
www.recchiuti.com

"When you introduce people to truly exquisite chocolate and ingredients, they will be won over instantly. That's the Recchiuti philosophy."

Tcho

Est. 2005 by Karl Bittong
and Timothy Childs
3100 San Pablo Avenue
Berkeley, CA 94702
Tel: 844-877-8246
www.tcho.com
FT

"We partner with cacao farmers, cooperatives, and cocoa research institutes around the globe, with the goal to produce the best cacao beans possible."

Ad for Phillips Digestible Cocoa (1891)

Colorado

Chocolove
Est. 1996 Timothy Moley
1880 S 57th Ct.
Boulder, CO 80301
Tel: 888-246-2656
www.chocolove.com
FT �*/

"Our chocolate factory… follows the classic European traditions of making chocolate in the mountains. Crisp, cool, dry air is one of many secret ingredients."

District of Columbia

Divine Chocolate
Est. 1990 by Sophi Tranchell
804 E Street, SE
Washington, DC 20003
Tel: 202-332-8913
www.divinechocolate.com
🍫 FT K

"Divine Chocolate is co-owned by the 85,000 farmer members…the cooperative in Ghana that supplies the cocoa….As owners, they get a share in the profits."

Florida

Garcia Nevett
Est. 2012 Susana and Isabel Garcia Nevett
7312 Red Road
Miami, FL 33143
Tel: 305-749-0506
www.garcianevett.com
🥾 V

"Susana and Isabel … have spent more than a decade perfecting their chocolatier skills…always celebrating Venezuelan cacao...and now infusing it with the flavors of South Florida."

Norman Love
Est. 2001 by Norman and Mary Love
11380 Lindbergh Blvd
Fort Myers FL 33913
Tel: 239-561-7215
normanloveconfections.com
🥾

"Norman Love has been producing beautiful handcrafted chocolate… with an emphasis on artistry, premium ingredients, and innovative flavor."

Georgia

Xocolatl

Est. 2014 by Elaine Read
and Matt Weyandt
99 Krog Street
Atlanta, GA 30307
Tel: 404-604-9642
www.xocolatlchocolate.com

"[We] make dark chocolate free of fillers & unnecessary ingredients but full of flavor ….With gratitude to the people & place that inspired us, we hope our chocolate brings you the same sense of contentment & adventure."

Hawaii

Lonohana

Est. 2009 by Seneca
Klassen
344 Coral Street
Honolulu, HI 96813
Tel: 808-286-8531
www.lonohana.com
FT

"We produce an…array of bars that incorporate organic Hawaii-grown inclusions… coffee, macadamia nuts, cacao nibs, sea salts, fruits and spices."

Manoa Chocolate

Est. 2010 by Dylan
Butterbaugh
333 Uluniu Street
Kailua, HI 96734
Tel: 808-753-1089
www.manoachocolate.com

"We started as college students with no money and bootstrapped our business with ingenuity and deter-mination…. we seek the highest quality beans from across the Hawaiian islands and around the globe."

Waialua Estate

Est. 1996 by David Murdock
64-1551 Kamehameha
Highway
Wahiawa, HI 96786
Tel: 808-372-6760
www.waialuaestate.com

"Waialua…cacao, grown along the banks of the Kaukonahua…the North Shore's rich, fertile, sweet soil, provides an exceptional terroir to the chocolate."

Idaho

Chocolat Bar
Est. 2003 by Jason Stack
805 W Bannock St.
Boise, ID 83702
Tel: 208-338-7771
www.thechocolatbar.com

"The quality and flavor of our chocolate is the foundation upon which our sophisticated offerings are built as we utilize our own unique chocolate blends."

D. GHIRARDELLI & CO.

ONLY

CHOCOLATE MANUFACTORY

IN CALIFORNIA.

Manufactory of Ground Coffee,

SYRUPS AND LIQUORS,

No. 415 Jackson Street.

6

Advertisement in the California Miner's Almanac (1854)

Illinois

Uzma
Est. 2011 by Uzma Shariff
1900 S. Halsted St.
Chicago, IL 60608
Tel: 312-674-6984
www.chocolat-uzma.com

"From our South Asian heritage to travels and experiences...we are always on the hunt for exciting spices and ingredients...to each chocolate."

Veruca
Est.2011 by Heather Johston
1332 N. Halsted St.
Chicago, IL 60642
Tel: 773-998-2462
www.verucachocolates.com
K

"I design each chocolate in a way that incorporates color, shape, pattern and texture to indulge all of the senses...that is what luxury chocolate is all about."

Vosges
Est.1998 by Katrina Markoff
2950 North Oakley Ave.
Chicago, IL 60618
Tel: 773-388-5560
www.vosgeschocolate.com

"We harness the power of storytelling to open minds, spirits and p=alates through esteemed chocolate, inspiring us all...."

Iowa

Stam
Est. 1913 by Jacobus Stam
2814 Ingersoll Ave.
Des Moines, IA 50312
Tel: 515-282-9575
www.stamchocolate.com

"Our family has been in the confectionary business for over 200 years....our current Master Chocolatier is the great, great, great, great, great grandson of our first baker."

Kansas

Hazel Hill
Est. 2006 by Nick and Terry Xidis
724 S. Kansas Avenue
Topeka, KS 66603
Tel: 785-215-8883
www.hazelhillchocolate.com

"Nick is the third generation chocolatier and...uses only the finest ingredients, chocolate, fresh cream and butter, to produce handmade treats that explode with flavor."

Kentucky

Amore di Mona
Est. 2011 by Mona Changaris
1201 Story Avenue
Louisville KY 40206
Tel: 502-532-8322
www.amoredimona.com

"As a longtime chocophile with a sensitivity to soy and nuts, I passionately enjoy creating and sharing beautiful, healthy chocolates with others."

Cellar Door

Est.2007 by Erika Chavez-Graziano
204 North 17th Street
Louisville KY 40203
Tel: 502-561-2940
cellardoorchocolates.com

"Erika's secret is that... taste is always most important. She ...uses a lot of unique flavor ...green chile coconut, dark chocolate licorice...white chocolate wasabi pea bark."

"The superiority of chocolate, both for health and nourishment, will soon give it the same preference over tea and coffee in America as it has in Spain."

-- Thomas Jefferson

Louisiana

Acalli

Est.2013 by Carol Morse
6104 Laurel St
New Orleans, LA 70118
Tel: 504-239-0845
www.acallichocolate.com
FT

"Great chocolate is a collaborative effort....The flavors... represent careful attention during cultivation, harvest, and especially fermentation and drying."

Maine

Ragged Coast

Est.2007 by Kate and Steve Shaffer
869 Main Street
Westbrook, ME 04092
Tel: 207-887-9763
raggedcoastchocolatiers.com

"We make all of our confections with fresh cream and butter from local farms ... herbs, fruits, vegetables, and edible flowers ...teas ...coffee... whole spices."

Maryland

Spagnvola
Est.2009 by Eric and
Crisoire Reid
360 Main Street
Gaithersburg, MD 20878
Tel: 240-654-6972
www.spagnvola.com

"We utilize only the finest beans grown from our estate in…the eastern part of the Dominican Republic…. Only the finest make their way to our artisan factory."

Velvet
Est.2010 by Ruthie Carliner
10403 Stevenson Road
Stevenson, MD 21153
Tel: 410-365-9883
thevelvetchocolatier.com
K

"Handmade chocolates with no preservatives, liquors, or added sugar, allows for the true flavor of the ganache to be experienced."

Massachusetts

Chequessett
Est. 2011 by Katherine
Reed and Josiah Mayo
8 Highland Road
North Truro, MA 02652
Tel: 774-538-6249
chequessettchocolate.com

"We carefully handcraft our chocolate in small batches from fine-flavor, sustainably grown cacao beans at our workshop on Cape Cod."

Chocolate Springs
Est.2003 by Joshua
Needleman
55 Pittsfield Rd
Lenox, MA 01240
Tel: 413-637-9820
www.chocolatesprings.com

"The mission of Chocolate Springs is to continue to spread and promote this time-honored, magical sensation of savoring exquisite chocolate."

Taza
Est.2005 by Alex Whitmore
and Kathleen Fulton
561 Windsor Street
Somerville, MA 02143
Tel: 617-284-2232
www.tazachocolate.com
FT K

"We stone grind organic cacao beans into perfectly unrefined, minimally processed chocolate with bold flavor and texture."

Ad for Baker's Cocoa of Massachusetts (1913)

Minnesota

Celeste
Est. 2001 by Mary Leonard
652 Transfer Road
Saint Paul MN 55114
Tel: 651-644-3823
www.chocolatceleste.com
FT

"Our confections are delicately made by hand with fresh heavy cream and small batch butter from local Minnesota farms. No preservatives. Ever."

Missouri

Askinosie
Est. 2005 by Shawn Askinosie
514 E. Commercial St.
Springfield, MO 65803
Tel: 417-862-9900
www.askinosie.com
FT K

"Askinosie Chocolate was born committed to fairness, sustainability, minimal environmental impact and community enhancement."

Christopher Elbow
Est. 2003 by Christopher Elbow
1819 McGee Street
Kansas City, MO 64108
Tel: 816-842-1300
www.elbowchocolates.com

"We do not use any preservatives or artificial flavors…We source local ingredients when we can and organic ingredients when we can."

Patric
Est. 2006 by Alan Patrick McClure
6601 Stephens Station Rd
Columbia, MO 65202
Tel: 573-814-7520
www.patric-chocolate.com
FT

"Patric…is an American craft chocolate company….we search the world for cocoa beans with the best flavor and choose organic whenever possible."

Rick Jordan
Est.2011 by Rick Jordan
14824 Clayton Rd
Chesterfield, MO 63017
Tel: 636-230-9300
www.rjchocolatier.com

"Experience the bold flavors of unique, artisan chocolates without the added chemicals and preservatives. We control the entire process."

Montana

Burnt Fork Bend
Est. 2007 by Jennifer Wicks
1072 Middle Burnt Fork Rd
Stevensville, MT 59870
Tel: (406) 370-8606
www.burntforkbend.com
🍫 FT

"My goal is to make the best tasting, highest quality chocolate using fair trade, minimally processed ingredients."

Posh Chocolat
Est. 2005 by Ana and Jason Willenbrock
111 North Higgins Avenue
Missoula, MT 59802
Tel: 877-544-7674
www.poshchocolat.com
V

"At the foot of the Rocky Mountains…Ana and Jason Willenbrock, husband and wife team, are… creating the most pure and highest quality chocolate."

Nevada

Jean-Marie Auboine
Est. 2012 by Jean-Marie Auboine
4780 West Harmon Ave.
Las Vegas, Nevada 89103
Tel: 702-222-0535
jmauboinechocolates.com
🍫

"Single-origin beans carefully selected from around the world and processed through a 12-step, bean-to-bar process, allows JMA to offer unique, one-of-a-kind tasting experiences."

New Hampshire

Dancing Lion
Est. 2007 by Richard Tango-Lowy
917 Elm Street
Manchester, NH
Tel: 603-625-4043
www.dancinglion.us

"I've learned to prepare her in the ancient ways of the Maya and in the gleaming kitchens of the finest Parisian chocolatiers…. Chocolate is my passion."

L.A. Burdick

Est. 1987 by Larry Burdick
47 Main Street
Walpole, NH 03608
Tel: 603-756-2882
www.burdickchocolate.com
V

"For more than three decades, we have been devoted to making our chocolates the time-honored way – by hand. …We cook, pipe, cut, dip, garnish, and pack our chocolates by hand."

New York

Antidote

Est. 2010 by Red
Thalhammer
173 Green Street
Brooklyn, NY 11222
Tel: 718-576-3995
www.antidotechoco.com
🍫 FT

"We are proud to offer dark and milk chocolate bars containing a higher cacao content and much less sugar than other brands…. With our formulas and slow roasting process we maximize antioxidants and nutrients."

Cacao Prieto

Est. 2010 by Daniel Prieto
Preston
218 Conover Street
Brooklyn, NY 11231
Tel: 347-225-0130
www.cacaoprieto.com
🍫 K 🍫

"Prieto was founded by Daniel Prieto Preston… whose family has been farming organic cacao in the Dominican Republic for more than 100 years."

Chocolat Moderne

Est. 2003 by Joan Coukos
Todd
27 West 20th Street
New York, NY 10011
Tel: 212-229-4797
www.chocolatmoderne.com
🍫 V

"Our fillings include numerous varieties of nuts and seeds …cocoa butter, cream, pure cane… fruit purees…citrus juices and zest, honey, liqueurs, essential oils, teas and spices."

Fruition

Est. 2011 by Bryan Graham
17 Tinker Street
Woodstock, NY 12498
Tel: 845-657-6717
fruitionchocolateworks.com
🍫 🍫 🍫 ✖ V

"Raised in France, Jacques fulfilled his American dream in 2000 with the opening of his first chocolate factory…in Brooklyn."

Ad for Huyler's Chocolate and Cocoa (1893)

Jacques Torres
Est. 2000 by Jacques Torres
350 Hudson Street
New York, NY 10014
Tel: 929-337-8856
www.mrchocolate.com
 K

"Raised in France, Jacques fulfilled his American dream in 2000 with the opening of his first chocolate factory…in Brooklyn."

Kreuther

Est. 2016 by Gabriel
Kreuther and Marc Aumont
68 35th Street
Brooklyn, NY. 11232
Tel: 212 924-2280
www.kreutherchocolate.com
K ⊠

"A true chocolate artist, Chef Aumont, along with his team, create inventive chocolates… rooted in classical French technique and inspired by traditional, yet surprising flavor combinations."

Li-Lac

Est. 1923 by George
Demetrious
68 35th Street
Brooklyn, NY. 11232
Tel: 212 924-2280
Li-LacChocolates.com
K ⊠

"Manhattan's oldest chocolate house …hand-crafted chocolate for almost 100 years. Using original recipes and old-world cooking methods."

MarieBelle

Est. 2001 by Maribel
Leiberman
484 Broome Street
New York, NY 10013
Tel: 718-599-5515
www.mariebelle.com

"From her first chocolate shop… Maribel's passion for discovering and sharing new flavors has seen her continually reinvent how we enjoy chocolate."

Oliver Kita

Est. 1996 by Oliver Kita
18 West Market Street
Rhinebeck, NY 12572
Tel: 845-876-2665
www.oliverkita.com
🌿 ν

"Heavy satin cream, award-winning sweet butter, the finest fruits, low sugar, and carefully selected and roasted nuts are all in an artfully hand-crafted design."

---

*"What is the meaning of life?
All evidence to date suggests it's
chocolate." -- anonymous*

Raaka

Est. 2011 by Ryan Cheney
64 Seabring Street
Brooklyn, NY 11231
Tel: 855-255-3354
www.raakachocolate.com
🍫 K 🍫 Y

"We make every bar from scratch with unroasted cacao beans, sourced from growers we trust and admire....Every recipe is inspired by the unique flavors of whatever bean we're working with.

North Carolina

Brasstown

Est. 2012 by Rom Still and Barbara Price
1151 Canal Drive
Winston-Salem, NC 27101
Tel: 336-818-8005
brasstownchocolate.com
🍫 FT 🍫

"Our love of chocolate art and ...the vast number of flavors attainable...have brought us to where are today. We love the entire chocolate making process."

Escazu

Est.2008 by Danielle Centeno
936 N. Blount Street
Raleigh, NC 27604
Tel: 919-832-3433
www.escazuchocolates.com
🍫

"The way we think of chocolate making...is not that of manufacturing a product but ...preparing food for family. With care, integrity and respect."

French Broad

Est. 2012 by Dan and Jael Rattigan
10 S. Pack Square
Asheville, NC 28801
Tel: 828-348-5321
frenchbroadchocolates.com
🍫 Y

"We roast, crack, winnow, grind, conche and temper chocolate in small batches...to elicit the best flavors each bean has to offer...our process continues to evolve."

Videri

Est. 2011 by Sam Ratto
327 W. Davie Street
Raleigh, NC 27601
Tel: 919-755-5053
viderichocolatefactory.com
🍫

"Videri...began as the shared dream of three chocolate lovers: Sam, Starr, and Chris....the chocolate factory is even more beautiful... than they had dreamt."

Ad for Dutch chocolate maker Van Houstens (1899)

Oregon

Creo

Est. 2007 by
122 NE Broadway
Portland, OR 97232
Tel: 503-477-8927
www.creochocolate.com

"We roast, crack, winnow, grind, conch and temper small batches of…beans and then mold and package each bar by hand. Our beans are sourced directly from the farmer."

Woodblock

Est. 2010 by Jessica and
Charley Wheelock
1715 NE 17th Ave
Portland, Oregon, 97212
Tel: 503-477-5262
woodblockchocolate.com

"Woodblock…the fortunate result of years of rigorous, artistic endeavors…by wife and husband team Jessica and Charley Wheelock…is like realizing a dream."

Pennsylvania

Alexandra & Nicolay

Est. 1993 by Alexandra and
Nicolay Mazhirov
507 Delaware Ave
Portland, PA 18351
Tel: 570-897-6223
alexandraandnicolay.com

"Alexandra and Nicolay start with the best base chocolate …and carefully craft their …products in a centuries- old Russian style."

Eclat

Est. 2005 by Christopher
Curtain
24 South High Street
West Chester, PA 19382
Tel: 610-692-5206
www.eclatchocolate.com

"Christopher honed his skills in…Belgium, Switzerland, France, Germany, and Japan… techniques that make eating Éclat…a unique experience."

John & Kira's

Est. 2007 by John and Kira
Doyle
163 West Wyoming Ave
Philadelphia, PA 19140
Tel: 800-747-4808
www.johnandkiras.com

"From…humble beginnings John and Kira's has grown and developed many… whimsical creations such as Chocolate Ladybugs…"

South Carolina

Christophe

Est. 2009 by Christophe and
Carly Paume
90 Society Street
Charleston, SC 29401
Tel: 843-297-8674
christophechocolatier.com

*"Christophe Paume is...a
third-generation French
chocolatier who grew up in
his father's pâtisserie...he
married Carly...and they
formed Christophe."*

Texas

Araya

Est. 2010 by Stefano Zullian
and Carla Susi
1575 W. Grand Parkway
S. Katy, TX 77494
Tel: 281-395-1050
www.arayachocolate.com
FT γ

*"Araya...is a family business
...Our chocolates are
handcrafted following the
French and Belgian techniques
using... Venezuelan
chocolate."*

Delysia

Est. 2014 by Nicole Patel
2000 Windy Terrace
Austin, Texas 78726
Tel: 512-413-4701
www.delysia.com
✉ K γ

*"Patel began handcrafting
chocolate truffles as a way to
relieve stress from her
engineering job. In a few
short years, she was named a
Top 10 Chocolatier."*

Kate Weiser

Est. 2014 by Kate Weiser
3011 Gulden Ln, Ste. 115
Dallas, Texas 75212
Tel: 512-469-619-4929
kateweiserchocolate.com

*"Kate has spent years
struggling to understand the
nuances of chocolates.... Her
handpainted chocolate
collection and artistic style
quickly gained attention...."*

Utah

Amano

Est. 2006 by Art Pollard and
Clark Goble
496 South, 1325 West
Orem, UT 84058
Tel: 801-655-1996
www.amanochocolate.com

*"Located high in Utah's
Wasatch Mountain range...
Amano is dedicated to
creating some of the world's
most exquisite chocolate...."*

Vermont

Lake Champlain
Est. 1983 by Jim Lampman
750 Pine Street
Burlington, VT 05401
Tel: 801-465-5909
lakechamplainchocolates.com
FT K

"From the first truffle in 1983...Vermont has inspired us to take a craftsman's approach to chocolate: creativity, patience, and mastery."

19th century ad for Whitman's Chocolate

Virginia

Gearharts

Est. 2001 by Tm Gearhart
243 Ridge McIntire Rd.
Charlottesville, VA 22903
Tel: 434-972-9100
gearhartschocolates.com

"After serving as a cook in the Marine Corps, Tim formally trained….returned to Charlottesville…crafting distinctive artisan chocolates."

Washington

Bellflower

Est.2012 by Will Dixon and Callie Neylan
1934 4th Ave West
Seattle, WA, 98119
Tel: 206-659-7053
bellflowerchocolate.com

"The Pacific Northwest is our home, the Olympic Mountains our muse. We are inspired by plants that provide us with chocolate…."

Forté

Est. 2006 by Karen Neugebauer
700 S 1st Street
Mt Vernon, WA 98273
Tel: 360-588-4859
www.fortechocolates.com
✍ Y

"We focus on bringing to life the…diverse flavors within pure chocolate and pairing it only with fresh, local cream and butter, adding only the finest …fruits, nuts, and spices…"

Theo

Est. 2005 by Joe Whinney
3400 Phinney Ave. North
Seattle, WA, 98103
Tel: 206-632-5100
www.theochocolate.com
FT ✍ K ✍ Y

"Theo's model is based on a core idea – chocolate can be made in a way that allows everyone in the bean to bar process to thrive."

Wisconsin

Tabal

Est. 2012 by Dan Bieser
7515 Harwood Avenue
Wauwatosa, WI 53213
Tel: 414-585-9996
www.tabalchocolate.com

K

"We love chocolate. The smell, the taste, the very thought of it. But it's chocolate's power to bring people together that fuels our passion…."

Wyoming

Meeteetse

Est. 2004 by Tim Kellogg
1943 State Street
Meeteetse, WY 82433
Tel: 307-868-2567
meeteetsechocolatier.com

"In June of 2004, my mother suggested that I make a bunch of truffles and brownies to sell…as a way to raise money….and that was that."

LATIN AMERICA

ARGENTINA

Nestled in the southwestern part of Argentina lies the beautiful town of San Carlos de Bariloche, known as "Little Switzerland" as a result of its culture, skiing, Alpine architecture, food – and most especially its chocolatiers. Many of them can be found along Mitre Avenue, otherwise known as the "Avenue of Chocolate Dreams." Below are some of these artisans:

Abuela Goye
Est.1981 by Luis Broger
Mitre 252
San Carlos de Bariloche
Tel: +54 294 442 9856
www.abuelagoye.com

"The name is a tribute to the first immigrant women …and pioneers, who with limited resources cooked rich and healthy in their new homes in Patagonia."

Del Turista
Est. 1964 by the Cecco Family
San Martin 252
San Carlos de Bariloche
Tel: +54 294 442 4725
delturistachocolates.com

"Everything began in 1940, in the Italian Tyrol…where the family Secco learned the trade of chocolatiers with the most ancient … Swiss-Italian Alps."

Frantom
Est. 2002 by Don Diego
Av. J.M.de Rosas y Panozzi
San Carlos de Bariloche
Tel: +54 9 294 452 2391
www.frantom.com.ar

"As worthy descendants of Italians, we have proudly assumed this heritage…. Our promise: Continue with … quality Patagonian artisanal chocolate."

Mamuschka
Est. 1989 by Juan Carlos Carzalo
Mitre 298
San Carlos de Bariloche
Tel: +54 294 442 3294
www.mamuschka.com

"Throughout our history, we have maintained the commitment to make products of excellence, with the best raw material, with the best processes."

Rapa Nui
Est. 1948 by Aldo Fenoglio
Mitre 202
San Carlos de Bariloche
Tel: +54 810 888 7272
chocolatesrapanui.com.ar

"Grandfather Aldo Fenoglio lived in Torino… working on the creation of fine delicacies of artisanal chocolate…. we hold with pride the old idea that he gave us."

Torres
Est.2008 by the Torres family
Mitre 222
San Carlos de Bariloche
Tel: +54 294 442 9315
www.chocolatestorres.com.ar

"Torres is a family business that invites you to enjoy the richest delights made with the subtlety and originality of its own chocolatier."

BARBADOS

Agapey
Est.2010 by Derrick Hastick
Cloister Bldg, Hincks Rd.
Bridgetown
Tel: 246-424-2739
www.agapey.com
🍫 FT

"Located in the hub of the Caribbean…this allows Agapey to…source beans from the best cocoa growing regions. We also use world renown, locally grown Barbadian gold cane sugar."

BELIZE

Cotton Tree
Est.2006 by Chris Crowell and Jeff Pzena
2 Front Street
Punta Gorda town
Tel: 501-621-8776
cottontreechocolate.com
🍫

"Cotton Tree Chocolate is a small batch chocolate. We are proud to be a product of Belize…Each batch…starts with cocoa beans from…a single farmer."

Mahogany

Est.2016 by David and
Debra Sewell
Mahogany Bay Village
San Pedro
mahoganychocolate.com

*"We produce premium
chocolate ...using special
cacao from our very own
"Peini" farms as well as ...150
Mayan cacao farmers in the
Toledo and Stann Creek."*

BOLIVIA

El Ceibo

Est.1977
Av. Juan Pablo II #2560
El Alto, La Paz
Tel: +591 284 1078
www.elceibo.com
FT

*"El Ceibo, committed to
protecting their native
rainforest, became the first
certified organic cocoa
cooperative in the world in
1988."*

Ancient drawing of Mayans before a cacao drink

BRAZIL

When cocoa first arrived to Brazil in 1746, it found an important place in the country's economy. By the early 1900s, Brazil ranked as the world's leading cocoa producer. Today, it still ranks highly, producing some 800,000 tons of chocolate per year, much of it in the state of Bahia. At the same time, Brazilians are buying more chocolate than ever. Once thought of as a special treat for holidays, it is now enthusiastically consumed all the year round, bringing with it a demand for high-quality chocolates such as these below:

Aquim
Est.2007 by Samanth Aquim
Rua Garcia D'Ávila, 149
Ipanema, Rio de Janeiro
Tel: +55 21 2274 1001
www.chocolateq.com

"The Q process, created and pioneered by the Aquim Family, allows the cocoa flavour to appear and flourish in its true identity…a tropical fruit."

Kopenhagen
Est. 1928 by David and Anna Kopenhagen
Rua D, Jose De Barros, 158
Centro – Sao Paulo - SP
Tel: +55 11 3257 8248
www.kopenhagen.com.br

"Kopenhagen…has as its mission: to manufacture products of the highest quality, preserving its flavor with sophistication and originality."

Mendoa
Est.2010
Av. Tancredo Neves, 620
Arvores Salvador - BA
Tel: +55 71 3014 1228
mendoachocolates.com.br

"Mendoá Chocolates are treasures conceived in the heart of the Brazilian Atlantic Forest…from cocoa beans…and…state of the art technology."

Nugali

Est.2004 by Maite Lang
and Ivan Blumenschein
R. Pres. Costa e Silva, 2250
89107-000 - Pomerode/SC
Tel: +55 47 3387 3468
www.nugali.com.br

"Made from a selected blend of cocoa and only the purest cocoa butter, Nugali chocolates are made just like the most traditional Belgian and Swiss chocolatiers."

CHILE

Damien Mercier

Est.1994 by Damien Mercier
Las Hualtatas 5176
Santiago, Vitacura
Tel: +56 2 2219 2702
www.damienmercier.cl

"Achieving perfection in chocolate is an art and a philosophy. We are dedicated to this...for more than 20 years....."

Entrelagos

Est.1976 by Montecinos- Kusch
and Birke-Engdahl families
El Rebellin Km. 10
Salida Norte, Valdivia
Tel: +56 6 321 2039
www.entrelagos.cl

"The ethnic flavors of Patagonia and northern Chile, blended with noble and traditional European ingredients, create the perfect synchrony."

Le Vice

Est.2013 by Jose Antonio
Carvallo
Av. Vitacura 3456
Santiago, Vitacura, Región
Metropolitana
Tel: +56 2 2823 6282
www.levicechocolat.com

"We use only the best ingredients....This is how we have achieved exclusive recipes that deliver a chocolate of excellence...."

Varsovienne

Est. 1954
Casa matriz Av. Einstein 787
Recoleta, Santiago
Tel: +56 2 672 67
www.varsovienne.cl

"With 63 years in the industry, our mission is to perpetuate the tradition, quality and exclusivity of our products...of our fine line."

COLOMBIA

With some of the finest cocoa beans, Colombian love of chocolate runs deep. Yet until recently, much of what was available were European brands. No more. Today, an explosion of local ones has hit the scene:

Me Late
Est. 2010 by Verónica Rendón
Carrera 36 # 8a 40
El Poblado, Medellin
Tel: +57 4 312 2363
www.melatechocolate.com
🍫 FT

"Me Late Chocolate is…warm, welcoming and full of love so that you relax, share and live a great experience around much, much chocolate."

Santander
Est. 1920
Carrera 52 2 38
Medellin
Tel: +57 1 8000 52 11 55
chocolatesantander.com
🍫

"Santander is origin chocolate produced in Colombia. Its name honors the name of the place where the best cacao in the country grows."

Colombia stamp featuring cacao

Suagu

Est.2016 by Maria Camila
and Juan Diego Suarez
Av. 19 No. 127B - 56
Bogotá
Tel: +57 310 881 6228
www.suagu.com

"Our mission; to make a chocolate of the highest quality, completely natural, nutritious and healthy, made with love."

Tibito

Est. 2015 by Gustavo Pradillo
Calle 97A No. 51-76
Bogotá
Tel: +57 1 635 0887
www.tibito.co

"We carefully created a top quality artisan chocolate by using the wonderful richness and great variety of the cocoa beans found in…Colombian regions."

COSTA RICA

The cacao bean has a significant role in Costa Rican history. Viewed as sacred by the Bribri and Chorotega people, it was a part of celebrations, used as currency, and was the country's leading export until others took the lead. Today, Costa Rica's cacao still fills its local producers with pride:

Caribeans

Est. 2006 by Paul Johnson
25 mets Oeste de Tasty
Puerto Viejo, Limón
Tel: 506 2750 0504
www.caribeanscr.com

"We are one of Costa Rica's first bean-to-bar companies with over ten years of cacao selection and chocolate making…all hand made."

Nahua

Est. 2011 Juan Pablo
Buchert
Plaza los Arcos L2
Heredia, Cariari 40703
Tel: 506 4702 7402
www.nahuachocolate.com

"Produced with unique single origin Trinitario cacao beans nurtured to their full-bodied flavor… through a meticulous post-harvest process."

Sibu

Est.2008 by Julio Fernandez
Amón and George Soriano
Apartado 308-3017
San Isidro
Tel: 506 2268 1335
www.sibuchocolate.com

"Inspired by cacao and chocolate's importance to our cultural history, we are working to bring back… chocolate making….into Costa Rica's future."

DOMINICAN REPUBLIC

Kah Kow

Est.1905 by Hector Rizek
Ave. Winston Churchill
Blue Mall, Santo Domingo
Tel: 809-955-3123
www.kahkow.com

 FT

"We have full control of the production from…the fruits to the final product. It is with great pride that we offer you this fine chocolate made by Dominican hands."

Xocolat

Est.1993 by Diana Munne
Manuel Emilio Perdomo, #19
Naco, Santo Domingo
Tel: 809-549-5036
www.xocolat.com.do

"Diana Munné, continuing the family tradition…makes handmade chocolates using the best organic cacao Hispaniola grown in the Dominican Republic."

"Chocolate comes from cocoa, which is a plant. Therefore, chocolate counts as salad." -- Anonymous

---

ECUADOR

Some of the earliest cocoa plants may have grown in the Ecuadorian Amazon, and there are signs that cocoa may have been consumed there as long as 4,000 years ago. But when Spanish conquistadors began exporting cocoa back to Europe, it was then that Ecuador made an international name for itself, becoming one of the world's largest exporters. While a devastating fungal infection hit its crops in the early 20th Century, the country has since made a huge comeback.

Hoja Verde

Est.2008 by Eduardo Letort
Valladolid N24-282 y
Francisco Galavis, Quito
Tel: 593-2-601-7050
hojaverdechocolate.com
K

"Our dream…is to produce the best possible chocolate …with differentiated varieties of cocoa…that connects the producer with the consumer."

Pacari

Est.2002 by Carla Barboto and Santiago Peralta
Zaldumbide N24-676 y
Miravale, Quito, Pichincha
Tel: 844-722-2274
www.pacarichocolate.com
K V

"Pacari works in small batches using…selected ingredients to bring you an unforgettable chocolate experience… all natural and 100% Ecuadorian."

Republica del Cacao

Est.2005 by the Chiriboga brothers
Avenida Colón y Yanéz
Pinzón, Edif El Dorado, Quito
Tel: +593 2-295-3161
republicadelcacao.com

"Our unique equatorial climate and rich, varied biodiversity provide the perfect conditions for growing cacao…."

Tavoro

Est.2014 by Katherine Coka
Jose Javanen N4-351
170802 Quito
Tel: 593 2 234 1549
www.tavorochocolate.com
🍫 K 🍃

"Our company was born from the initiative of… women, passionate about Ecuador, who are searching to provide the world…with the finest aromatic chocolate."

Ecuador stamp featuring cacao (1930)

EL SALVADOR 🏴

Xocolatisimo

Est.2015 by Victor Avelar
Blvd. del Hipodromo 548
Colonia San Benito
Tel: 503 2263 8649
www.xocolatisimo.com.sv
🍫

"Xocolatísimo takes … 100% Salvadoran chocolate and the expertise of the European tradition, to carry out the entire process to finish in a fine chocolate."

GRENADA

Jouvay

Est.2001
Diamond Street
Victoria St. Marks
Tel: 473-437-1839
www.jouvaychocolate.com

"Jouvay is one of a handful of chocolate producers around the world that have set up production facilities in the developing nation where our cocoa grows."

GUATEMALA

Present-day Guatemala is among those nations of the Meso-American region where chocolate was born – passed down from the Olmecs to the Mayans who then shared it with such European travelers as Italian Antonio Carletti who brought word back to the Medicis. Now, a new generation of chocolate makers are presenting their creations to the world:

Danta

Est.2008 by Carlos Eichenberger
10 Calle 0-65 Zona 14
Cent. Comercial Verdever #7
Tel: 502 2363 0100
www.dantachocolate.com

"We combine splendid Guatemalan cacaos with meticulous… techniques to obtain a finished product…in the highest spheres…of gourmet artisan chocolate."

Junajpu

Est.2010
5 Ave, Sur Final Antigua
Guatemala 03100
Tel: 502 5052 7044
www.junajpo.com

"Our mission…is to bring the ancestral flavor and magic of Guatemalan Cacao to as many people as we can throughout the Planet!"

HAITI

Askanya
Est.2015 by Corinne
Joachim-Sanon
75, Rue Espagnole
Ouanaminthe, Nord-Est
Tel: 509-34-87-6820
www.askanya.ht

"Askanya is Haiti's first and only premier bean-to-bar chocolate company....Our cacao is planted with upmost care in Haiti. For the cacao trees to thrive, they need moisture and plenty of rain."

JAMAICA

Chocolate Dreams
Est.2004 Michelle Smith
Shop 2A, 26 Hope Road
Kingston 10
Tel: 876-906-1173
chocolatedreams.com.jm

"As a young company producing everything in chocolate...we create handmade chocolates especially for our clients...We think Chocolate!"

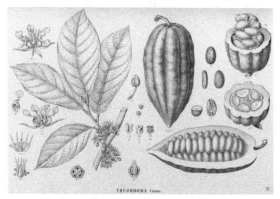

Cacao Drawing (1836)

MEXICO 🇲🇽

Among the earliest traces of chocolate consumption can be found in the Mayan civilization where it was ground and mixed with such spices as chili pepper and served warm as a drink for celebrations or health. The traditions were passed on to Aztecs who shared it with Spanish conquistadors in the 1500s led by Don Cortes. Today, Mexian chocolate continues to find new and ever more delicious formulations as shown here:

Johfrej
Est.2020 by Elvira Villasenor
Jesus 2A, Zona Centro
37700 S. Miguel de Allende
Tel: 52 415 152 3191
www.johfrej.com
☒

"We are a family company… preserving the recipes of our grandmother Elvira….The cocoa used for…our chocolate comes the state of Tabasco."

Kaokao
Est.2007
1a. Bis Sur
Cozumel, QR 77670
Tel: +52 1 987 119 7903
chocolateskaokao.com
🍫

"We are a family operated business dedicated to the creation of handmade Mexican chocolate…we are passionate about what we do."

Le Camelon
Est.2003 by Sophie Vanderbecken
Manuel Payno 87, Obrera,
06800 Ciudad de México
Tel: +52 55 5578 0141
lomejordelchocolate.com

"Our chocolate is as unique, as our history: with flavors, textures and processes forged and perfected through three generations of Belgian chocolatiers."

Vanuato
Est.1991 by Fabiola Palma
Homero 425-B, Polanco
Mexico D.F. C.P. 11570
Tel: 52 55 5233 0333
www.vanuatokakaw.com

"Our products are made with the finest choice of natural ingredients, thus preserving its exquisite taste and incomparable smoothness."

NICARAGUA

Momotombo
Est.2004 by Sonia Moraga,
Carlos Jose Mann
Plaza Altamira Mod.#2
Managua
Tel: 505-2270-2094
www.momotombochocolate
factory.com

"Momotombo…is a small artisanal bean to bar operation that produces a diverse range of chocolates made exclusively with Fine Nicaraguan Cacao."

PERU

Amaz
Est. by the Morales family
C.A. Izaguirre Mz M lote 6
San Martin de Porres, Lima
Tel: 511 250 2597
www.amazfoods.com.pe
FT

"We are firmly committed to acting with social and environmental responsibility throughout the entire chain of operations."

Marana
Est.2015 by Zulema Leon
and Giuseppe Cassinelli
Las Magnolias NRO. 207
Dpto, 502 Lima-Barranco
Tel: 511 340 9861
www.marana.com.pe

"Our..chocolates are made with the finest selection of Peruvian cocoa beans from three different regions of Peru: Cusco, Piura and San Martin."

Shattell
Est.2010
Calle Montegrande 120
Surco, Lima
Tel: 511 624-9244
www.shattell.com

"Organic chocolates with 'criollo' cocoa from different areas of the Peruvian Amazon region, recognized around the world for its excellent flavor."

VENUZUELA

El Rey

Est.1929 by Jose Rafael
Zozaya and Carmelo Tuozzo
Calle 5 con Calle 7, Parcela
B3-01, La Urbina, Caracas
Tel: 58 212-2427738
www.chocolateselrey.com
FT

*"Since its foundation in
1929...we are...dedicated to
transform the best cocoa in
the world to exceed the
expectations of our
consumers."*

Franceschi

Est.1830 by Vicente
Franceschi Vicentelli
El Paisa, Avenida Caroní
Caracas 1060
Tel: 58 212-9510398
franceschichocolate.com

*"A unique collection of dine
and extra-fine chocolates,
made from selections of
ancestral Venezuelan cacao
of Criollo and Trinitario
Origin."*

ASIA, MIDEAST, & AFRICA

AUSTRALIA

Australians love chocolate! According to the latest statistics, they are eating more and more of it -- buying it not just as a gift for others but simply for themselves. Luckily, the cacao plant is able to grow there too, mostly in the Daintree rainforest in far-north Queensland. Among local chocolatiers are such longstanding stalwarts as Haigh's as well as plenty of enterprising newcomers like some of those below:

Bahen
Est.2009 by Josh Bahen
P.O. Box 2012
Margaret River WA 6285
Tel: +61 8 9757 1034
www.bahenchocolate.com
🍫 FT

"Chocolate can only be as good as the quality of the cacao....We spend a lot of time searching for these rare varieties of heritage cacao... taking a simplistic approach to respect flavour."

Haigh's
Est.1915 by Alfred Haigh
153 Greenhill Rd, Parkside
South Australia, 5063
Tel: +61 8 8372 7000
haighschocolates.com.au
🍫

"We're very proud to be "The oldest family-owned chocolate maker in Australia....Our cooking processes … use meticulous artisan skills...."

Jasper + Myrtle
Est. 2016 by Li Peng Monroe
Garran, Canberra, 2605
Tel: +61 416 182 477
jasperandmyrtle.com.au
🍫

"All … chocolates are handmade from cacao beans...from Peru and Papua New Guinea...with a focus on allowing the flavor... to come through."

Koko Black
Est.2003 by Shane Hills
52 Collins Street
Melbourne VIC 3000
Tel: +61 3 9663 556
www.kokoblack.com

"The Koko Black range is complex, indulgent, and always adventurous…. Each individual chocolate is meticulously crafted here in Melbourne."

Monsieur Truffe

Est.2006 by Thibault Fregoni
351 Lygon St, Brunswick E.
Victoria 3056
Tel: +61 3 9380 4915
monsieurtruffechocolate.com

"We created a huge range of bars and delights suitable for vegan and gluten free diets, all whilst not compromising on quality."

Zokoko

Est.2008 by Michelle Morgan
84–90 Old Bathurst Road
Emu Heights NSW 2750
Tel: 1300 965 656
www.zokoko.com

"My dream is to make amazing, unique chocolate reflective of its origin…. Zokoko's bean to bar process was designed to celebrate chocolate in every way."

FIJI

Fijiana

Est.2007 by Tomohito and
Harumi Zukoshi
Denarau Industrial Park
Denarau Island, Nadi
Tel: 679 672 1011
www.fijianacacao.com

"It is our wish to show the world how very beautiful Fiji chocolate is….We revitalized our soulful cacao trees and began to process some of the finest dark chocolates."

HONG KONG

Vero

Est.2004 by Roger Chan
6/F Sun Hing Industrial Bldg
46, Wong Chuk Hang Road
Tel: 852 2559 5838
www.verochocolates.com

"Vero is on a continuous quest to bring impeccable quality…. Our delicacies are handmade every day by a team of passionate

INDIA

Mason & Co
Est.2014 by Jane Mason
and Fabien Bontems.
Fraternity, Auroville, Vanur
Taluk, Villupuram District,
Tamil Nadu 605101
Tel: +91 8940 559 024
www.masonchocolate.com

"We are proud to say we execute every step in this unique process...We work closely with organic farmers to source only the best quality organic cacao beans."

Pristine
Est.2008
XV-519, Moozhikkulam
Kurumassery P O, Aluva
Kerala 683579
Tel: +91 93875 32483
www.pristinechocolates.com

"We make all our own chocolate, from bean to bar, the way all chocolate should be made! ...Our factory is situated in the cocoa farm itself, a rare scenario in the world..."

INDONESIA

In this fourth-most-populous nation, local chocolate brands dominate, aided by locally grown cocoa beans of which there are plenty. Indonesia is actually the third-largest producer in the world. Today, Indonesians, whose incomes are rising, are welcoming in newer chocolatiers.

Krakakoa
Est. 2013 by Sabrina
Mustopo and Simon Wright
Jl. Ikan Mas Gudang Lelang
No.46, Kangkung, Bumi
Waras, Bandar Lampung
Tel: +62 21 2270 7031
www.krakakoa.com

"Founded in 2013...we wanted to make it clear ... our chocolate is proudly Indonesian....cacao beans are organically-grown and sourced from small farms."

Monggo

Est.2001 by Thierry Detournay
Jl. Dalem KG III / 978
Kel. Purbayan Kotagede
55173 Yogyakarta
Tel: +62 274 37 3192
www.chocolatemonggo.com

"Production takes place in …Kotagede where our handmade delights are created….continuously working… to improve our products with respect for all."

Pod Bali

Est.2010 by Toby Garritt
Jl Sunset Road 89
Kuta Bali 80361
Tel: +62 361 849 6228
www.podbali.com

"Our beans come from freshly harvested pods and often become chocolate within days of being on a tree."

ISRAEL

Cardinal

Est.2006 by Elie Tarrab
60 Ibn Gabirol St
Tel Aviv
Tel: 972-3-695-8612
www.cardinaltlv.com

"Located in the heart of Tel Aviv…we produce small batches, therefore, our customers enjoy the freshness and aroma of the chocolates."

Ika

Est.2011 by Ika Cohen
11 Yad Haruzim Street
Tel Aviv
Tel: 972-3-688-0440
www.ikachocolate.com

"Ika is passionate about using the finest ingredients in the traditional techniques ….True to her homeland spirit, Ika is committed to innovation."

"Nobody knows the truffles I've seen."
-- *unknown*

JAPAN

When you think of Japanese chocolate, picture delicately crafted pieces that are almost like works of art. That is what you will find among the dedicated artisans who are thriving there today – and quickly making a name for themselves around the world, winning some of the top international prizes.

Es Koyama

Est.2003 by Susumu Koyama
5 Chome-32-1, Yurinokidai,
Sanda, Hyōgo 669-1324
Tel: 81 79-564-3192
www.es-koyama.com

"Susumu…has attracted attention throughout the world in the field of chocolate…. He continues to develop a professional taste … with a sense of high quality."

Green Bean to Bar

2-16-11 Aobadai
Meguro-u, Tokyo 153-0042
Tel: 81 3 5728 6420
www.greenchocolate.jp

"Our products are made by hand, in small batches…..we focus on quality rather than speed and volume. We are perfectionist and pay attention to every detail."

Minimal

Est.2014 by Takashi Yamashita
2-1-9 Tomigaya, Shibuya
151-0063, Tokyo
Tel: 81 3-6322-9998
www.mini-mal.tokyo

"Minimal…manages all processes (selection, roasting, grinding, blending, molding) from cocoa beans to making plate chocolate in our own studio."

Palet d'Or

Est. 2004 by Shunsuke Saegusa
100-0005 Tokyo, Chiyoda,
Marunouchi, 1 Chome-5-1
Tel: 81 3-5293-8877
www.palet-dor.com

"Palet d'Or…has a Bean to Bar studio that handles all processes from cocoa beans to chocolate."

Vanilla Beans

Est.2000 by Katsuhisa Yagi
5 Chome-25-2 Kaigandori
Naka Ward, Yokohama
Tel: 81 45-319-4861
vanillabeans.yokohama
🍫 FT

"We make chocolate to make everyone - including those who eat, make, and grow it - smile. We go to great lengths to thoroughly sustain using the finest ingredients."

LEBANON

Elsa Chocolatier

Est.1994 by the Karout family
Burj el Murr, Beirut
Tel: +961 1 375983
www.elsachocolatier.com
🍫

"Elsa Chocolatier Boutique redefines customers' interaction with chocolate, making it more intimate and immersive...."

Patchi

Est. 1974 by Nizar Choucair
Patchi Building, Weygand St.
Beirut Central District
Tel: +961 1 982888
www.patchi.com

"At Patchi...We pride our-selves in using the highest quality cocoa butter, cocoa mass, sugar and milk. No colorings or preservatives are used."

Drawing of cacao plant (1880)

MADAGASCAR

Chocolaterie Robert
Est.1940 by the Robert family
472 Blvd. Ratsimandrava
Soanierana, Antananarivo
Tel: 261 20 22 205 65
chocolaterierobert.com

"In recent years, Chocolaterie Robert has focused its transformations on the aromatic diversity of cocoas according to the terroirs of the country, and also according to the seasons."

Menakao
Est. 2005 by Shahin Cassam Chenai
Lot 288F 93 Ambohitsara
Antananarivo, 105
Tel: 261 20 22 535 23
www.menakao.com

"Menakao develops specially adapted recipes and selects the best beans ...dark chocolate recipes are vanilla-free to enhance the natural aromas...."

MALAYSIA

Beryl's
Est. 2003 by Ting Sii Liong
No. 2, Jalan Raya 7/1
K. Perindustrian
43300 S. Kemb., Selangor
Tel: +60 38 943 6136
www.berylschocolate.com

"We...are passionate...to produce the finest quality of chocolates by combining traditional techniques with modern technology."

Chocolate Concierge
Est. 2015 by Ong Ning Geng
Bangsar Shopping Centre
59000 Kuala Lumpur
Tel: +60 12 528 2562
www.chocconcierge.com

"Chocolates are freshly crafted within days and made locally. This is key because nuts, fruits or dairy components taste the best ...when they are fresh."

NEW ZEALAND

Hogarth
Est. 2014 by Karl and Marina
Hogarth
10F Kotua Place Stoke
Nelson 7011
Tel: +64 3 5448623
hogarthchocolate.co.nz

"Our small factory is located in Nelson…where we sort, roast, crush and classify, winnow, grind and conche, age, melt, temper, mold, and wrap by hand."

Makana
Est. 1998 by Jim and Debi
Makaweo
504 Kerikeri Road
Kerikeri, Bay of Islands
Tel: +64 9 407 6800
www.makana.co.nz

"We start with the best possible ingredients…. We make all of our products by hand in small batches. We also hand pack all of our products by hand."

Patagonia
Est. 2005 by Alex Gimenez and
Lorena Giallonardo
P.O. Box 1067
Queenstown, 9348
Tel: +64 3 441 2891
patagoniachocolates.co.nz

"A longing for the exquisite chocolate of their Argentinian homeland led owners Alex Gimenez and Lorena Giallonardo to establish Patagonia…."

Detail from the "La Xocolatada" tiled painting (Barcelona, 1710)

PHILIPPINES

While Filipinos are not unique in their love of chocolate, their fondness that stands out when, for example, one comes upon the array of chocolate products in a local supermarket or in the impressive display of chocolatiers below:

Auro

Est. 2015 by Mark Ocampo and Kelly Go
Davao City
Davao del Sur
Tel: +63 82 296 6768
www.aurochocolate.com
🍫 FT ⚥ �

"Auro...is a proudly Filipino, bean-to-bar chocolate company that sustainably sources our cocoa beans directly from local farming communities."

Hiraya

Est. 2015 by Arvin Peralta
106 FBR Arcade, Katipunan Avenue, Quezon City
Tel: +63 235 53714
hirayachocolates.com
🍫 FT

"We make single-origin chocolate bars ... from cacao beans sourced around the Philippines ....We are...an advocate of sustainable...practices."

Malagos

Est. 2003 by Roberto and Charita Puentespina
#57 Mother Ignacia St. Bgry Paligsahan, Quezon
Tel: +63 2 929 9310
malagoschocolate.com
🍫

"We have been in agriculture for over three decades.... We produce chocolate that is proudly Philippine.... that is truly tree-to-bar."

Risa

Est. 2017 by Pamela Lim Cinco
CRM Ave, Almanza Dos Las Pinas, Metro Manila
Tel: +63 918 942 4573
www.risa.ph

"What started as an exercise in joy, shared with family and friends, has grown into a chocolate company that imbues the same passion and joy."

Theo and Philo

Est. 2010 by Philo Chua
610 Asuncion Street
Binondo 1000 Metro Manila
Tel: +63 2 242 4093
www.theoandphilo.com

FT Ⓥ

"Each batch of chocolate is produced in small quantities …. from the selection of the cacao bean to the final step of molding and packing, we only offer the best we can."

SAO TOME ★★

Claudio Corallo

Est. 1995 by Claudio Corallo
Av. 12 de Julho nº 978
CP 678 São Tomé
Tel: 239 222 2236
www.claudiocorallo.com

"The cultivation of the bean and the production of the chocolate always go hand in hand whereby we aim for the highest possible quality."

Diogo Vaz

Est. 2014 by Jean-Remy Martin
1001 Ave. Marginal 12 Julho
São Tomé
Tel: +33 6 85 37 96 06
diogovazchocolate.com

"There is no shortcut with cacao....It is a very precise and delicate crop....Our vision is to focus on the ones with greatest organoleptic qualities such as the Amelonado."

"Chocolate is cheaper than therapy, and you don't need an appointment."

-- unknown

SINGAPORE

Fossa
Est. 2016 by Jay Chua,
Yilina Leon, Charis Chia
10 Tuas Baywalk #02-22
Singapore 637780
www.fossachocolate.com

"Inspired by a new generation of chocolate makers worldwide, we are in pursuit of bringing forth the wonderful flavours of cacao to our neighborhood."

Laurent Bernard
Est. 2006 by Laurent
Bernard
The Pier at Robertaon Quay
#01-11 Singapore 239013
Tel: 65 9725 0579
laurentbernard.com.sg
✉

"What started as an exercise in joy, shared with family and friends, has grown into a chocolate company that imbues the same passion and joy."

SOUTH AFRICA

De Villiers
Est. 2009 by Pieter de Villiers
Suid-Agter Paarl Road
Paarl
Tel: +27 21 874 1060
www.dvchocolate.com

"To make our chocolate from the cocoa bean …allows us to develop our own unique flavour profiles as we control all the critical processes...."

Honest
Est. 2009 by Michael de
Klerk and Anthony Gird
66 Albert Road
Cape Town
Tel: +27 21 447 1438
honestchocolate.co.za

"We believe in keeping things handcrafted, using old school methods, using quality organically produced ingredients, and making a pure chocolate that has a deliciously distinct feel and taste."

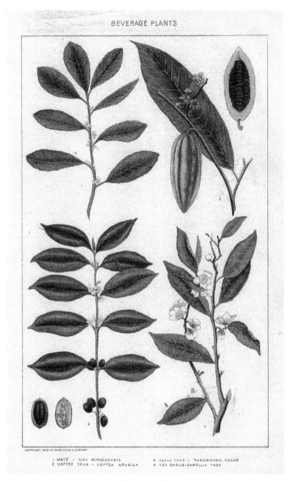

Maté, coffee, cocoa, and tea plants (1902)

Afrikoa

Est. 2010 by the Karera and
Allegra families
2b Elegance Road
Sanddrift, Cape Town 7441
Tel: +27 21 551 1806
www.afrikoa.com

"We combine only the finest naturally organic, heirloom cocoa beans with locally-grown unrefined cane sugar to create our range of chocolates – no gluten, soy, GMO's, palm oil or artificial flavourings or colourings."

SOUTH KOREA

P. Chokko

Est. 2016 by Dan and Jon Kim
685-315 Seongsu-dong 1(il)ga
Seongdong-ju, Seoul
Tel: +82 2 512-0565
www.pchokko.com

"Jon and Dan grew up in a fusion of cultures, making the brothers natural connoisseurs of distinctive tastes and flavors....to find the highest level."

TAIWAN

Yu

Est. 2015 by Yu Hsuan Cheng
No. 10, Alley 3, Lane 112,
Section 4, Ren'ai Road,
Da'an District, Taipei City
Tel: +886 2 2701 0792
www.yuchocolatier.com

"Yu Chocolatier…is a brand new perspective of the Asian Flavor, delicate in flavor, adventurous in soul, a beautiful marriage of Asia and Occident."

Fu Wan

Est. 2015 by Warren Hsu
No.100 Dapeng Rd.
Donggang Township
Pingtung
Tel: +886 8 835 1555
www.fuwanshop.com

"I only buy our fresh cacao pods from Taiwanese farmers …. Each step is carried out by myself and my handpicked team…as we bring to market a tree-to-bar chocolate."

UNITED ARAB EMIRATES

Mirzam
Est. 2016 by Kathy Johnston
73 6 Street
Dubai
Tel: +971 4 3335888
www.mirzam.com

"Using granite wheels, the roasted beans are ground for several days in a process which slowly decreases the molecule size to create incredibly smooth chocolate."

VANUATU

Aelan
Est. 2013 by Sandrine Wallez
P.O. Box 5125
Port-Vila, Efaté
Tel: +678 22554
www.aelanchocolate.com

"Aelan was born from a passion for cocoa and artisanal manufacturing and in the aim to create a new market for the local cocoa producers to improve their…livelihoods."

VIETNAM

Marou
Est. 2011 by Vincent Mourou and Samuel Maruta
169 Calmette street
Ho Chi Minh City
Tel: 84 283 729 2753
www.marouchocolate.com

"Somehow, the country's fine flavored cacao remained hidden for over a century. When we found it, we quickly understood that we could make great chocolate."

CHOCOLATE FESTIVALS

For those who *really* like chocolate, below are some festivals you can attend in your city or perhaps on your next vacation. Listed to the right is the month when the festival is typically held.

Australia

Chocolate Winterfest   August
www.chocolatewinterfest.com.au

Smooth Festival of Chocolate   August
smooth.com.au/smooth/festival-of-chocolate

Belgium

Salon du Chocolat (Brussels)   March
http://brussels.salon-du-chocolat.com

Brazil

Expo Brasil Chocolate   Sept
www.expobrasilchocolate.com.br

Canada

Chocolate Fest (New Brunswick)   August
http://chocolate-fest.ca/newsite/

Toronto Chocolate Festival   November
www.torontochocolatefestival.com

France

Salon du Chocolat (Paris)   November
www.salon-du-chocolat.com

Italy

CioccoArtSicily www.cioccolartsicily.it	November
CioccoLentino (Terni) www.cioccolentino.com	February
Festa del Cioccolato di Bologna www.cioccoshow.it	November
Fiera del Cioccolato (Florence) www.fieradelcioccolato.it	March

Japan

Salon du Chocolat www.salon-du-chocolat.jp	January

Mexico

Salon Chocolate www.tradex.mx/chocolates/	August

Netherlands

Chocoa Festival www.chocoa.nl	February

UNITED STATES

Alabama

Mobile Chocolate Festival www.mobilechocolatefestival.com	March

Arkansas

Eureka Chocolate Lovers' Festival www.eurekachocfest.org	February

California

Ghirardelli Chocolate Festival www.ghirardelli.com/chocolate-festival	September

Colorado

Colorado Chocolate Festival   May
www.chocolate-festival.org

Holiday Chocolate Festival   December
www.holidaychocolatefestival.com

Delaware

Wilmington Wine & Chocolate Festival   February
www.ghirardelli.com/chocolate-festival

Florida

Fairchild Chocolate Festival   January
www.fairchildgarden.org

Pensacola Chocolate Fest   April
www.pensacolachocolatefest.com

Hawaii

Big Island Chocolate Festival   April
www.bigislandchocolatefestival.com

Illinois

Galesburg Chocolate Festival   April
galesburghistoricalsociety.com/chocolate_fest

Illinois

Galesburg Chocolate Festival   February
galesburghistoricalsociety.com/
chocolate_fest

Indiana

Chocolate Fest Indy   April
www.chocolatefestindy.com

Kentucky

Chocolate Fest (Louisville)   September
www.chocolatefestlouisville.com

Massachusetts

Harvard Square Chocolate Festival   January
www.harvardsquare.com

Salem's So Sweet Chocolate Festival   February
www.salemmainstreets.org/festivals

New Mexico

Southwest Chocolate and Coffee Fest   March
www.chocolateandcoffeefest.com

New York

Chocolate Expo   December
www.thechocolateexpo.com

I Love Chocolate Fest   March
www.lovechocolatefest.com

New Mexico

Southwest Chocolate and Coffee Fest   March
www.chocolateandcoffeefest.com

Nevada

Las Vegas Chocolate Festival   April
www.lasvegaschocolatefestival.com

North Carolina

Carolina Chocolate Festival   February
www.carolinachocolatefestival.com

Oregon

Oregon Chocolate Festival   March
www.oregonchocolatefestival.com

Pennsylvania

Lititz Chocolate Walk   October
www.oregonchocolatefestival.com

Tennessee

Chocolatefest Knoxville   January
www.chocolatefestknoxville.com

Texas

Dallas Chocolate Festival   September
www.dallaschocolate.org

Washington

Chocolate on the Beach Festival   February
www.chocolateonthebeachfestival.com

Northwest Chocolate Festival   November
www.nwchocolateo.com

West Virginia

Lewisburg Chocolate Festival   April
www.lewisburgchocolatefestival.com

Wisconsin

Burlington Chocolate Festival   May
www.chocolatefest.com

CHOCOLATE GLOSSARY

Arriba – A mild-flavored variety of forastero cocoa bean grown in Ecuador.

Cacao – The name of both a tropical tree and its bean which is found in the tree's pods and is used to make chocolate.

Chocolate Liquor – A paste produced when cacao beans are roasted and ground, and used as a baking ingredient.

Cocoa Butter – The fat which is removed from the cacao bean.

Cocoa Powder – The resulting product after fat has been removed from the cacao bean.

Conching – The process of kneading chocolate paste in a machine in order to bring out its flavor and texture.

Couverture – very high-quality, glossy type of chocolate used to cover or decorate pieces of fruit or other items.

Criollo – The rarest of the three types of cocoa beans, it originated in Central America and has a more complex flavor.

Dutch Cocoa – Chocolate that has been treated with an alkalizing agent to modify its color and give it a milder taste.

Fermentation – A process of exposing the cocoa bean to air and yeast which helps develop its flavor.

Forestero – The most common of the cocoa beans, it grows in both Africa and the Americas.

Ganache – a mixture of chocolate and cream used to fill the center of truffles or as a filling in cakes or tarts.

Grinding – a mechanical process of crushing the roasted cocoa bean nib, resulting in the chocolate liquor.

Nib – The center of the cacao bean, which is roasted and ground into cocoa mass (chocolate liquor).

Praline – a type of confection containing nuts and sugar and sometimes cream.

Roasting – a part of the chocolate-making process which darkens the cocoa bean and further brings out its flavor.

Tempering – The final step of the chocolate-making process which gives the chocolate a more even, uniform sheen.

Theobroma Cacao – The botanical name first given to the cacao tree in 1753 by Swedish naturalist Carl Linnaeus.

Trinitario -- This cocoa bean is a hybrid of the other two varieties (criollo and forestero) and has a full-bodied flavor.

Truffles – A round confectionery with ganache at its center coated in chocolate, cocoa powder or chopped toasted nuts.

White Chocolate – Made from a blend of cocoa butter, milk solids, sugar, milk fat and lecithin – but no chocolate solids.

Winnowing – The process of removing the outer husk of the cacao bean in order to extract the nib inside.

COCOA, FAIR TRADE & SUSTAINABILITY

Be a happy and responsible chocolate eater!
Learn more about these organizations:

Fair Trade Certified
1500 Broadway, Ste 400
Oakland, CA 94612
Tel: 510-663-5260
www.fairtradecertified.org

International Cocoa Initiative
Chemin de Balexert 9
1219 Châtelaine | Switzerland
Tel: +41 22 341 47 25
www.cocoainitiative.org

Raise Trade
Rural Business Centre
Myerscough College, Bilsborrow
PR3 0RY United Kingdom
Tel: +44 1995 642159
www.raisetrade.com

World Cocoa Foundation
1411 K Street NW, Suite 500
Washington, D.C. 20005, USA
Tel: 202-737-7870
www.worldcocoafoundation.org

World Cocoa Farmers Organization
Savannahweg 17, 3542 AW
Utrecht, The Netherlands
Tel: +31 3027 65110
www.worldcocoafarmers.org

CHOCOLATE IN
95 LANGUAGES

Afrikaans – sjokolade
Albanian – cokollate
Amharic - ቸኮላት
Arabic - شوكولاتة
Armenian – շոկոլադ
Azerbaijani - şokolad

Basque – txokolatea
Belarusian – шакалад
Bengali - চকলেট
Bosnian – čokolada
Bulgarian – шоколад

Catalan – xocolata
Chichewa – chokoleti
Chinese -巧克力
Croatian – čokolada
Czech – čokoláda

Danish – chokolade
Dutch – chocola

Esperanto – ĉokolado
Estonian – šokolaad

Filipino – tsokolate
Finnish – suklaa
French – chocolat
Frisian – chocolat

Galician – chocolate
Georgian - შოკოლადი

German – Schokolade
Greek – σοκολάτα
Gujarati - ચોકલેટ

Haitian – chokola
Hausa – cakulan
Hawaiian – kāleka
Hebrew – שוקולד
Hindi – चॉकलेट
Hungarian – csokoládé

Icelandic – súkkulaði
Indonesia – cokelat
Irish – seacláid
Italian – cioccolato

Japanese - チョコレート
Javanese – coklat

Kannada - ಚಾಕೊಲೇಟ್
Kazakh – шоколад
Khmer - សូកូឡា
Korean –초콜릿
Kurdish – çîkolata
Kyrgyz – шоколад

Laos - ຊັອກໂກແລດ
Latin – scelerisque
Latvian – šokolāde
Lithuanian – šokoladas

Macedonian – чоколада
Malagasy – sôkôla
Malay – coklat
Malayalam - ചോക്കലേറ്റ്
Maltese – ċikkulata
Maori – tiakarete
Marathi - चॉकलेट
Mongolian – шоколад
Myanmar - ချောကလက္

Nepali - चकलेट
Norwegian – sjokolade

Pashto – چاکليټ
Persian – شکلات
Polish – czekolada
Portuguese – chocolate
Punjabi - ਚਾਕਲੇਟ

Romanian – ciocolată
Russian – шоколад

Samoan – sukalati
Scotts Gaelic – seoclaid
Serbian – чоколада
Sesotho – tsokolate
Sindhi – چاڪليٽ
Slovak – čokoláda
Slovenian – čokolada
Somali – shukulaatada
Spanish – chocolate
Sundanese – coklat
Swahili – chokoleti
Swedish – choklad

Tajik – шоколад
Tamil - சாக்லேட்
Telugu - చాక్లెట్
Thai – ช็อคโกแลต
Turkish – çikolata

Ukranian – шоколад
Urdu – چاکليٹ
Uzbek – shokolad

Vietnamese - sô cô la

Welsh – siocled

Xhosa – tshokoleji

Yiddish – שאָקאָלאַד
Yoruba – chocolate

Zulu – ushokoledi

ALPHABETICAL INDEX

Green & Black's	48
Guido Gobino	34
Guittard	55

H

Haigh's	89
Handgjort	43
Hazel Hill	59
Hazel Mountain	31
Heindl	15
Hiraya	100
Hogarth	99
Hoja Verde	84
Honest	102
Hotel Chocolat	48
Hummingbird	50

I

Iain Burnett	48
Idilio	46
Ika	95

J

Jacek	51
Jacques Torres	66
Jasper & Myrtle	92
Jean-Marie Auboine	64
Jean-Paul Hévin	26
Johfrej	88
John & Kira's	70
John Kelly	49
Jordi's	21
Joulietta	20
Jouvay	86
Junajpu	86

K

Kah Kow	83
Kaokao	88
Kate Weiser	71
Koko Black	92
Kopenhagen	79

Krakakoa	94
Kreuther	67
Kyya	52

L

L.A. Burdick	65
Laderach	45
Lake Champlain	72
Laurent Bernard	102
Le Camelon	88
Le Vice	80
Leonidas	18
LetterPress	54
Li-Lac	67
Lily O'Brien's	32
Lonohana	57
Lorge	32
Lulu's	56
Lyra	40

M

Mahogany	78
Maison du Chocolat	26
Makana	99
Malagos	100
Malmo	43
Mamuschka	76
Manoa	57
Marana	89
MarieBelle	67
Marou	105
Mary	18
Mason & Co	94
Max	45
Me Late	81
Menakao	98
Meeteetse	74
Mendoa	79
Mercedes	22
Minimal	96
Mirzam	85

Momotombo	89
Monggo	95
Monsieur Truffle	93
Montezuma's	48

N

Nahua	82
Naïve	35
Neuhaus	19
Norman Love	56
Nugali	80

O

Oberweis	35
Oialla	21
Oliver Kita	67
Omnom	31
Original Beans	37
Oriol Balaguer	42

P

P. Chokko	104
Pacari	84
Palet d'Or	96
Patagonia	99
Patchi	97
Patric	63
Patrick Roger	26
Paul A. Young	48
Peter Beier	21
Pierre Hermé	26
Pierre Marcolini	20
Pod Bali	95
Posh	64
Pralus	27
Pristine	94
Puccini Bomboni	39

R

Ragged Coast	60
Rapa Nui	77

Recchiuti	54
Republica del Cacao	84
Richart	27
Rick Jordan	63
Risa	100
Roberto Catinari	34
Rózsavölgyi	30

S

Santander	81
Schokov	15
Sebastien Bruno	38
Shattell	89
Sibu	83
Simon Coll	42
Slitti	34
Soma	53
Spagnvola	61
Sprungli	45
Stam	59
Suagu	82
Sucr'elle	85
Summerbird	22
Svenningsen	22

T

Tabal	74
Tavoro	85
Taza	61
Tcho	54
Teuscher	45
Theo	73
Theo & Philo	101
Thomas Haas	51
Tibito	82
Torres	77

U

Uzma	58

SPECIALTY INDEXES

Brands listed below may offer at least *some* (though not necessarily all) products adhering to these standards. To be certain about a specific item, please check with the chocolatier directly.

Bean to Bar

Erithaj	26	Lonohana	57
Es Koyama	96	Lulu's	54
Escazu	68	Lyra	40
Favarger	44	Mahogany	78
Feitoria do Cacao	40	Malagos	100
Fijiana	93	Malmo	43
Fossa	102	Mamuschka	76
Franceschi	90	Manoa	57
French Broad	68	Marana	89
Fruition	65	Marou	105
Fu Wan	104	Mason & Co.	94
Gay-Odin	34	Me Late	81
Goodio	22	Menakao	98
Goosens	18	Mendoa	79
Green & Black's	48	Minimal	96
Grean Bean to Bar	79	Mirzam	105
Guido Gobino	34	Momotombo	89
Guittard	53	Monggo	95
Hachez	18	Monsieur Truffle	93
Haigh's	92	Nahua	82
Hazel Mountain	31	Naïve	35
Hiraya	100	Nugali	80
Hogarth	99	Oialla	21
Hoja Verde	84	Omnom	31
Honest	102	Original Beans	37
Hotel Chocolat	48	P. Chokko	104
Hummingbird	50	Pacari	84
Idilio	44	Palet d'Or	96
Jacek	51	Patagonia	99
Jacques Torres	66	Patric	63
Jasper & Myrtle	92	Paul A. Young	48
Jean-Paul Hévin	26	Peter Beier	21
John & Kira's	70	Pierre Marcolini	20
Jordi's	21	Pod Bali	95
Jouvay	86	Pralus	27
Junajpu	86	Pristine	94
Kallari	24	Raaka	68
Kah Kow	83	Republica del Cacao	84
Kaokao	88	Rick Jordan	63
Krakakoa	94	Robert	76
Kyya	52	Rogue	16
LetterPress	54		

Santander	81
Shattell	89
Sibu	83
Simon Coll	42
Slitti	34
Soma	53
Spagnvola	61
Suagu	82
Tabal	74
Tavoro	85
Taza	61
Tcho	54
Theo	73
Theo & Philo	101
Tibito	82
Vanilla Beans	97
Venchi	35
Videri	68
Villars	35
Vivani	29
Waialua Estate	57
Wilkie's	32
Woodblock	70
Xocolat (Dom.)	83
Xocolatisimo	85
Xocolatl	57
Yu	104
Zak's	52
Zokoko	93
Zotter	16

Fair Trade

Acalli	60
Agapey	77
Amaz	89
Antidote	65
Araya	71
Askinosie	63
Auro	100
Bahen	92

Belvas	17
Bouga	25
Brasstown	68
Burnt Fork Bend	64
Celeste	63
Chocolatemakers	37
Chocolove	56
Dagoba	19
Divine	56
Dolfin	18
Domori	34
El Ceibo	78
El Rey	90
Fossa	102
Fruition	65
Green & Black's	48
Guittard	53
Heindl	15
Hiraya	100
Hummingbird	50
Jacek	51
Junajpu	86
Kah Kow	83
Kyya	52
Lake Champlain	72
Lulu's	54
Malmo	43
Me Late	81
Montezuma's	48
Original Beans	37
Patric	63
Puccini Bomboni	37
Taza	61
Tcho	54
Theo	73
Theo & Philo	101
Van Soest	37
Vanilla Beans	97
Zokoko	93
Zotter	16

Gluten Free

Amore di Mona	59
Askinosie	63
Auberge du Chocolat	46
Auro	100
Belvas	17
Caffarel	33
Casa Kakau	20
Choc on Choc	47
Chocolat Moderne	65
Chocolate Bar	58
Chocolatemakers	37
Choklat	50
Christopher Elbow	63
Compartes	53
Delysia	71
Fossa	102
Garcia Nevett	56
Haigh's	92
Heindl	15
Hotel Chocolat	48
Jacques Torres	66
John Kelly	54
Junajpu	86
Lulu's	54
Max	45
Mercedes	22
Monsieur Truffle	93
Montezuma's	48
Norman Love	56
Puccini Bomboni	37
Raaka	68
Ragged Coast	60
Shattell	89
Tabal	74
Taza	61
Theo & Philo	101
Velvet	61
Xocolatl	57
Zak's	52
Zotter	16

Kosher

Askinosie	63
Belvas	17
Bonnat	24
Cacao Prieto	65
Chocolove	56
Delysia	71
Divine	56
Genaveh	35
Hoja Verde	84
Jacques Torres	66
John Kelly	54
Lake Champlain	72
Leonidas	18
Li-Lac	67
Max	45
Neuhaus	19
Pacari	84
Raaka	68
Tabal	74
Tavoro	85
Taza	61
Theo	73
Velvet	61
Veruca	58

Organic

Amore di Mona	59
Acalli	60
Alexandros	30
Amaz	89
Askinosie	63
Belvas	17
Belyzium	28
Blanxart	41
Bouga	25
Brasstown	68
Caribeans	82
Casa Kakau	20
Cacao Prieto	65

Sugar-Free

Vegan

Araya	71	Max	45
Auberge du Chocolat	46	Mercedes	22
Auro	100	Mirzam	105
Belvas	17	Monsieur Truffle	93
Beta5	50	Oliver Kita	67
Casa Kakau	20	Pacari	84
Choc on Choc	47	Posh	64
Chocolat Moderne	65	Puccini Bomboni	37
Chocolatemakers	37	Raaka	68
El Ceibo	78	Ragged Coast	60
Forte	73	Soma	51
Fossa	102	Tabal	74
French Broad	68	Theo	73
Garcia Nevett	56	Vosges	59
Gluten Free	72	Xocolatl	57
Green & Black's	48	Zak's	52
Heindl	15	Zotter	16
Hotel Chocolat	48		
Hummingbird	50		
Junajpu	86		
L.A. Burdick	65		
Lulu's	54		

Is there a chocolate brand you love and would like to recommend?

Please write to us at: listings@ grahamesguides.com.